MODERN
NATIONS
—OF THE—
WORLD

HAITI

MODERN
NATIONS
—OF THE—
WORLD

HAITI

BY EMILY WADE WILL

LUCENT BOOKS
P.O. BOX 289011
SAN DIEGO, CA 92198-9011

Library of Congress Cataloging-in-Publication Data

Will, Emily Wade.
   Haiti / by Emily Wade Will.
      p.   cm. — (Modern nations of the world)
   Includes bibliographical references and index.
   ISBN 1-56006-761-6 (alk. paper)
   1. Haiti—Juvenile literature. [1. Haiti.] I. Title.   II. Series.
F1915.2 .W55 2001
972.94—DC21

00-009884

CONTENTS

INTRODUCTION

HAITI: A NATION DARING DEFINITION

Nanpounin maladi ki pa gin rémèd.
There's no sickness that doesn't have a remedy.
(There's always a way out.)
— Edner A. Jeanty and O. Carl Brown,
Parol Granmoun: Haitian Popular Wisdom

Haiti is a puzzle, a country of perplexing paradoxes, of contradictions. To follow its history is to negotiate a labyrinth of odd twists and turns. It is a small slice of Africa amid mostly Latin, Spanish-speaking cultures; the Dominican Republic, Cuba, and Puerto Rico are among its nearest neighbors. Once Europe's wealthiest colony, with the great powers vying to wrest it from France, Haiti is now one of the poorest nations on Earth. It has been home to a gentle indigenous people, to gold-hungry conquistadors, to depraved buccaneers, to plantation owners corrupted by wealth and power, and to former slaves whose greatest desire was always to own some land and to be left alone to farm it.

Born of the first and only major slave revolution to give rise to an independent nation, Haiti quickly became bogged down in class distinctions based on skin color. And however proud of their hard-won independence, for all practical purposes Haitians have been enslaved since then by some of the world's most abusive dictators—sons and grandsons of slaves themselves.

Haiti's peasants have had what their counterparts throughout Latin America have wanted but have been denied: their own land. Rather than ending up self-sufficient in food production, however, the Haitian people are hungry on a land that has become an ecological disaster. Its soil, once the source of the colony's immense wealth, is now depleted. Peasants must struggle to wrestle the barest of harvests from it.

The tragedy of Haiti is that its people, despite their abundance of shared culture and experience, have created distinctions that drive them into opposing groups. The culture that Haitians share is genuinely unique and rich, but it does not bind the population together. Instead, the commonalities are overshadowed by class divisions, based largely on skin color differences, which may be imperceptible to outsiders.

Together on their tiny spot on the globe, Haitians endure the regular ravages of hurricanes and the intermittent wrenchings of earthquakes. They share a unique, exquisitely expressive language. Vodun, their religion, is also unique in the world—a true melding of African beliefs and Roman Catholicism molded during years of isolation. Rich and poor Haitians alike have suffered equally under intolerable tyrants. Yet none of this common experience has been sufficient to overcome the wide gulf separating the small elite from the impoverished masses.

Despite their nation once being the Caribbean's most prosperous area, today Haitians struggle to obtain life's basic necessities.

1

LAND AND PEOPLE

Moun ki pa mange pou kò-l pa janm grangou.
Those who share with others always have something
to eat.

— Edner A. Jeanty and O. Carl Brown,
Parol Granmoun: Haitian Popular Wisdom

Haitians value sharing. Perhaps this is because of their West
African heritage, which emphasizes the community rather
than the individual. Perhaps it is because the country is so
impoverished that most people could not survive if they did
not share. Whatever the case, it is a valuable ethic for a people who must share even the small island on which they live
with another country. The island, named Hispaniola, com-
prises both Haiti and the Dominican Republic.

THE LAND

Hispaniola is the second-largest island in the Caribbean Sea.
It is sandwiched between Cuba and Jamaica on the west and
Puerto Rico on the east. The island somewhat resembles a
short, squat alligator with its mouth agape. Haiti is the alligator's head and jaw—about one-third of the island. Port-au-
Prince, the nation's capital, sits at the point where the two
jaws meet, along the Golfe de la Gonâve.

Haiti, though part of a small island itself, possesses five
tiny islands of its own. Île de la Gonâve looks like a slender
fish that the alligator is about to gulp down. A smaller second
island, Tortuga, resembles a luckier turtle that escaped above
the opened jaw. Even more petite are the islands of Vache,
Les Cayemites, and La Navase. While the islands do not hold
any special importance to Haiti today, Tortuga Island played
a pivotal role in Haiti's history. Tortuga served as the home
base for French hunters-turned-pirates. The pirates' occu-
pancy of the island, and of the northwestern corner of Hispaniola, was sufficient to allow France to claim and obtain
the western third of Hispaniola from its original European
owner, Spain.

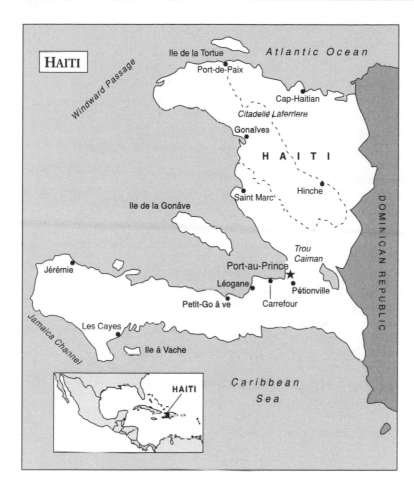

The name *Haiti* comes from one of several words that the indigenous people who first met Christopher Columbus, the Taíno Arawaks, used for their country. That word was *Ayiti*, which means "Mountainous." About two thirds of Haiti is mountainous. Historians frequently repeat the story that when French emperor Napoléon Bonaparte was scheming to retake Haiti in 1801, he asked about its topography. An officer crumpled a piece of paper, dropped it, and said, "That, Sire, is the terrain."[1]

Mountains still define Haiti. The country's few roads are in disrepair, and the rough terrain hinders transportation and communication between the coastal cities and the inland villages. It is a bone-jarring five-hour Jeep ride from the capital of Port-au-Prince to an inland village no more than 110 kilometers (68 miles) away. Haiti's highest peak is Morne La

COLUMBUS MEETS THE TAÍNO

Christopher Columbus kept a detailed log of his journeys to the New World. This passage, excerpted and condensed from entries dated December 7–26, 1492, is from a translation by Robert H. Fuson, published in *The Log of Christopher Columbus*, and tells of his first meeting with the Taíno people.

[These] are some of the most beautiful plains in the world, almost like the lands of Castile [a large region of Spain], only better. Because of this, I have named this island *La Isla Española* [the Spanish Island]. I placed a large cross at the entrance to the harbor. This is a sign that Your Highnesses [Spain's Queen Isabella and King Ferdinand] possess this land as your own and especially as an emblem of Jesus Christ, our Lord, and in honor of Christianity.

[A young woman] showed us the location of [a Taíno] village. She wore a small piece of gold in her nose, which is an indication that there is gold in this island. The village consisted of more than 1,000 houses. [The inhabitants] all went to their houses and brought the bread of *niamas* [manioc], which are tubers [roots] and look like large radishes. These are planted in all their fields and are their staff of life.

Your Highnesses may believe that . . . all that is needed here is to build a town and order the Indians to do your bidding. [They] have no knowledge of arms and are very timid. So they are suitable to be governed and made to work and sow and do everything else that shall be necessary, to build villages and be taught to wear clothing and to observe our customs.

They are an affectionate people, free from avarice [greed] and agreeable to everything. I certify to Your Highnesses that in all the world I do not believe there is a better people or a better country. They love their neighbors as themselves, and they have the softest and gentlest voices in the world and are always smiling. The King maintains a most marvelous state, where everything takes place in an appropriate and well-ordered manner.

Christopher Columbus

Selle at 2,638 meters (8,793 feet). As researcher Wade Davis has pointed out, Haiti's mountains create "an illusion of space that absorbs Haiti's multitudes."[2]

But Haiti's 27,856 square kilometers (10,714 square miles)—an area roughly the size of Maryland—consist of more than mountains. "Rarely can one find such utter diversity in a small space as in Haiti," writes author James G. Leyburn. "Dull wastes of salt marshes; arid deserts where cactus grows, spiked and hairy, to enormous heights; canyons, waterfalls, dried-up streams; moors, little jungles, farms; rich plantations of sugar cane, dusty stretches of sheer barrenness."[3]

In the mostly dry country, one of Haiti's most highly valued geographical features even today is the Artibonite River. Some 278 kilometers (174 miles) long, the Artibonite River runs through central Haiti from east to west, emptying into the Golfe de la Gonâve. The second-largest river, Les Trois Rivières, meanders for a mere 96 kilometers (60 miles). None of Haiti's rivers is deep or wide enough for commercial shipping; only small crafts such as canoes can travel them.

The Artibonite River provides water to the central Artibonite Valley, a plain on which most of Haiti's crops—principally rice—are produced. This valley is often referred to as Haiti's breadbasket. Other rich farmland is found on a few plains extending from the mountains to the coast, such as the Plaine du Nord, near the northern coastal town of Cap Haitien.

A less desirable geographic feature is a long fault line that traverses Haiti's length just south of Port-au-Prince. Due to this fault line, the country experiences periodic seismic activity. For example, earthquakes destroyed Port-au-Prince in 1770 and Cap Haitien in 1842.

THE CLIMATE

Haiti's mountains play a large role in determining climate. The temperature of a village located 1,480 meters (4,700 feet) above sea level averages sixteen degrees Celsius (sixty degrees Fahrenheit) annually. People living higher in the mountains may see an occasional frost. Sea-level temperatures are considerably warmer. Port-au-Prince residents, for example, enjoy an average yearly temperature of twenty-six degrees Celsius, (seventy-nine degrees Fahrenheit).

Haiti's tropical climate is considerably drier than that of its neighbor, the Dominican Republic, because mountains in eastern Haiti cut off the trade winds—winds that blow steadily to the equator from the northeast—and the rains they bring. Much of Haiti's northwest peninsula (the "upper jaw") and Île de la Gonâve are arid. Some regions are plagued by periodic drought, which gives rise to famine. However, other parts of the country are usually wet at least part of the year. In these regions, the rainy season can occur anytime from April to November and typically lasts two to three months.

Haiti's mountains, now mostly deforested, play a vital role in determining the nation's climate.

Sometimes the rains come packaged in a fury. The southern peninsula (the "lower jaw") for example, is particularly vulnerable to hurricanes. The horrific destruction of Hurricane Hazel in 1954 still remains in older Haitians' memories. Authors Robert Debs Heinl Jr. and Nancy Gordon Heinl vividly describe the disaster:

> On 11 October 1954, howling over slate-gray seas, eighty-knot [about 92 miles per hour] winds lashed up from the south. Hurricane Hazel hit the [southern] coast at Port-à-Piment, ripped viciously past Cayes, all but destroyed Jérémie, leveled villages, killed at least a thousand victims, denuded 40 percent of Haiti's coffee bushes, flattened irretrievably the new [government-] sponsored banana plantations, and uprooted half the country's cacao trees. Nan Mapou, a prosperous village outside Port-à-Piment, was converted into a mile-long lagoon. Malaria and sickness stalked Hazel's wake.[4]

Nine years later, in 1963, Hurricane Flora killed five thousand people, left one hundred thousand homeless, and in the south, it wiped out 95 percent of the cattle and more than half the coffee crop. Hurricane Cleo whisked in the following year, followed by Hurricane Inez in 1966. Inez also killed thousands of people and practically razed the large town of Jacmel on the southern coast.

In 1980 Hurricane Allen blasted Haiti's southwest peninsula, destroying up to 10 percent of all houses and inflicting heavy crop damage. Hurricane Georges in 1998 was unusual in that it first rammed the central Artibonite Valley rather than the southern peninsula. Some two hundred people died, thousands of houses were severely damaged, crops were lost, and tens of thousands of farm animals were killed. The flooding that came along with Hurricane Georges affected people throughout the country, including Port-au-Prince residents.

NATURAL RESOURCES

These periodic tempests further ravage a country that is largely depleted of natural resources. "Natural resources: none."[5] That is the starkly simple entry about Haiti in the *World Factbook 1999*, published by the U.S. Central Intelligence Agency. Haiti was not always bare of natural resources, however. At one time its most valuable resources were fertile lands and lush forests of lignum vitae, mahogany, pine, rosewood, and other prized species.

Unlike its once-abundant renewable resources, Haiti was not endowed with many nonrenewable natural resources. Its small stores of bauxite—the ore used to make aluminum—were extracted by Reynolds Metals Company between 1953 and 1983. Companies have drilled for oil in the Golfe de la Gonâve, but to date none has been found. Haiti must therefore import oil. Additionally, the country's one hydroelectric dam, located on the Artibonite River, produces only about 40 percent of the electricity now used in Haiti.

More recently, new gold and copper reserves have been found in the northeast, but they are presently too costly to extract. This is because Haiti possesses almost no infrastructure, or system of roads, communication, power plants, and other basic community facilities. Such infrastructure is needed if large mining corporations with titan-size machinery are to operate as needed.

Although Haiti has never been blessed with abundant mineral or oil deposits, its fertile land was once a treasure that allowed crops to flourish. In the middle to late 1700s, this rich land made Haiti so agriculturally productive that it became France's wealthiest colony, a sparkling jewel in the European nation's crown. Indigo, sugar, coffee, and cacao flourished, and French plantation owners in Haiti, which was then known as Saint Domingue, lived liked royalty. In 1791 Haiti's exports to France totaled some $41 million. "Rich as a West Indian planter"—the West Indies being another name for the Caribbean islands—became a common saying in Paris and other European capitals to describe anyone wealthy enough to spend freely and live in luxury.

Since the country gained its independence in the early 1800s and the plantation system came to an end, however, the great majority of Haitians have lived as subsistence farmers, growing crops—such as corn, rice, sorghum, millet, manioc, yam, plantain, fruits, and vegetables—for family consumption on their own land. As the population grew, parents divided their plots among their children, who then divided their holdings among their offspring.

THE TAÍNO, A PEACEFUL PEOPLE

The Taíno Arawak had lived on many of the Caribbean islands for nearly six hundred years when Europeans first arrived in the New World. When Christopher Columbus landed at Hispaniola in 1492, the Taíno were thriving. An estimated 1 million Taíno were living peacefully on the land, cultivating a starchy root crop called manioc, which they made into bread, their staple food. With what they grew, hunted, and fished, they had plenty to eat all year round.

The Taíno had divided Haiti into at least five provinces, and an all-powerful leader, similar to a king or queen, ruled each province. These leaders were called caciques. The provinces, in turn, were divided into districts and villages.

A typical village consisted of two hundred to five hundred Taíno families. A plaza served as the village center, and the leader's home faced the plaza. A husband, wife, and two or three children made up an average family. As many as fifteen families, perhaps all related, lived together in large windowless one-room houses. These round homes were sturdily constructed of thick wooden posts supporting circular thatch walls and roofs.

The Taíno enjoyed recreation, often participating in games and festivities in the village plaza. Teams of men and women competed in a sport called *batey*. The object of the game was to keep a rubber ball in the air—and in the court—by hitting it using only shoulders, elbows, hips, and knees. No hands or feet were allowed!

At festivals, the Taíno celebrated with songs and dances called *areytos*. A leader would begin an *areyto*, and participants would repeat the leader's words and copy the leader's steps. Through their *areytos*, the Taíno passed along various tales and legends.

At various times governments also allotted government-owned land, often former plantations, to retiring soldiers to pay them for their service. These new owners also divided up their land among their children. Gradually, almost all of Haiti has become splintered into tiny plots. Today Haitian farmers often own or rent two to four little fields, usually located far enough apart from one another that they must walk for hours to reach their fields.

In the eighteenth century, Haiti's fertile soil made it France's most valuable colony.

Holdings became so small that, in order to grow enough food to feed their families, peasant farmers began to clear trees from hill- and mountainsides to create additional farming space. They did this without necessarily owning or renting the land, simply taking it over by using it, or "squatting" on it. Rural residents also cut trees for firewood and to make charcoal—the country's preferred cooking fuel—by partially burning logs in underground pits.

With the trees gone, little remains to anchor the soil. Today rain continues to flush much of Haiti's topsoil into the ocean, greatly decreasing the land's ability to produce crops. To make up for skimpier harvests on such depleted land, farmers try to find yet more land to farm, creating a vicious

A group of girls play jump rope in Port-au-Prince. Nearly half of Haiti's population is under fifteen years old.

cycle that continues to encourage deforestation. Some farmers are even cultivating mountain slopes so steep that they must secure themselves with rope at the waist before descending to tend their plots.

THE POPULATION

Despite the obstacles farmers face, they did manage—up until about the 1980s—to produce enough food to support an ever-growing population. Haiti has long been one of the world's most densely populated countries, and in 1998 the World Bank estimated the country's total population at 7.6 million. It is a young population, with 43 percent under fifteen years of age. A mere 4 percent is over age sixty-five.

Writing about his first visit to Haiti in the mid-1950s, author Herbert Gold commented, only partly in jest, that Haiti "was so densely populated, even then, that the visitor found it difficult to relieve himself by the side of the road without a crowd of peasants materializing out of the brush to observe his achievement."[6] Haiti's population then was 3.5 million, less than half of what it is now.

Most Haitians—at least 90 to 95 percent—share direct ancestry to the 480,000 African slaves who won their freedom from France in 1804. Most of the remaining 5 to 10 percent of Haitians share at least part of the African blood of Haiti's early slaves. But the latter group, known as mulattos, identifies more with its French ancestors—white colonists—than with the black slave women with whom its forefathers sired children.

Since Haiti's founding, the divide between Haiti's mulattos and poor blacks has been at the root of many of the nation's greatest ills. According to the Heinls, "This racial division—Haitians call it exactly that and speak of 'the two races'—is the most important fact of life in Haiti. It dominates the country's whole existence. It is also, in the words of one of Haiti's ablest thinkers, Alcius Charmant, '. . . the supreme evil of our Republic, the virus that ravages it, and the road to its ruin.'"[7]

The mulattos became Haiti's ruling class, its elite. Living in urban areas, mainly Port-au-Prince, this group has held—and continues to hold—the lion's share of Haiti's power and wealth. Although members of the elite grow up learning the French dialect Kreyòl (also known as Creole) from their nannies and servants, they speak French among themselves and usually go abroad for schooling.

While the elite reside in modern homes or villas with servants to wait on them, drive luxury cars, and even jet to Miami to go shopping, Haiti's masses struggle to survive day by day. At least three-fourths of Haitians live in abject poverty, earning less than $150 a year. Almost one in ten children born in Haiti dies before reaching age one. Safe drinking

KREYÒL

Although all Haitians speak Kreyòl, only recently is the language coming into its own as one of Haiti's official tongues. Members of Haiti's elite have traditionally distanced themselves from their poor black cousins by learning and speaking French. But even the wealthiest Haitian also learns Kreyòl from nannies, maids, gardeners, and even relatives.

Kreyòl was born of the French spoken by hunters living on Tortuga Island during the 1600s, and it was seasoned by English, Spanish, Caribbean, and African influences. From this "soup pot" bubbled a unique language, with vocabulary more French than African, with sounds and cadence more African than French, and a simplified structure or syntax owed to its English influence.

water is available to only 13 percent of the population. A mere 20 percent of Haitian children finish primary school, and only 25 percent of Haitian adults can read and write.

RURAL HAITI

Flying over Hispaniola east to west, travelers can easily see when the plane has crossed the border from the Dominican Republic into Haiti. The luxuriant green mountains of the Dominican Republic abruptly end, replaced with Haiti's bald, brown mountain humps. The majority of Haitians still try to eke out a living on land picked so clean of vegetation that some have called it a moonscape. Because of the lack of habitat, little wildlife remains.

"You can read about deforestation and its effects in the books and pamphlets written by [foreign] experts, and then you can read about it in the faces and bodies of Haitian peasants," notes journalist Amy Wilentz.

> The bloated bellies and orange hair of the children of the Northwest are chapters in a long book about the failed bean crop, the persistent drought, the pitiful corn harvest, the lack of green pasture for livestock. The bony arms and legs of the mountain women, and their skeletal babies, are passages about the lack of water in the countryside, and testimony to drinking water that is stagnant, infested. The tough sinews and concave stomachs of the day workers, and their meals and snacks that consist of clairin [cheap rum] and more clairin, are the summation of a story of dry earth.[8]

The rural areas have been home to the large majority of Haitians, but the government has largely ignored these areas—except to collect taxes. Few paved roads go into the hinterlands—Haiti has just 1,011 kilometers (627 miles) of paved roads—and families farm and market much as they did a hundred or even two hundred years ago. Farm implements include hoes, machetes, and human muscles. Women employ large wooden pestles—clublike implements used with strong vessels called mortars—to pound grain while standing outside their tiny straw-thatched huts.

Without public transportation in the countryside, people create makeshift stretchers using tree branches and chairs to carry the infirm to one of the country's few hospitals or clinics. To transport nearly everything else, Haitians either balance items atop their heads or load them onto the backs of donkeys. Writer Wade Davis colorfully describes this "You-Haul" method in which just about anything imaginable

> is carried on the head—baskets of eggplant and greens, bundles of firewood, tables, a coffin, a single piece of [sugar] cane, sacks of charcoal, buckets of water, and countless unidentifiable drab bundles. Everything large or small is carried atop out of habit as much as necessity, like a delightful but defiant challenge to the laws of gravity.[9]

CITIES

Since its founding, Haiti has been predominantly a rural nation, traditionally with 80 to 85 percent of its people living in the countryside. Due to the political and economic upheaval of the late twentieth century, as well as the bleak difficulties facing subsistence farmers, migration to towns and cities has accelerated. The 1999 *World Almanac* classified 32 percent of Haitians as urban; other sources estimate an urban population as high as 40 percent.

Port-au-Prince, Haiti's capital and largest city, teems with some 2 million people and grows at an annual rate of 8.5 percent. As Haiti's only major city, it dominates the country's political, cultural, and economic activities. Davis captures the overall flavor of the capital with this description:

> Port-au-Prince is a sprawling muddle of a city, on first encounter a carnival of civic chaos. A water-front shanty-town damp with laundry. Half-finished, leprous public monuments. Streets lined with *flamboyant* [trees with showy crimson flowers] and the stench of fish and sweat, excrement and ash. Dazzling government buildings and a presidential palace so white that it doesn't seem real. There are the cries and moans of the marketplace, the din of untuned engines, the reek of diesel fumes.[10]

Recently, rural Haitians have also begun relocating to Cap Haitien, the country's second-largest municipality, although it still more resembles a large town than a city. Other major towns that are growing as people leave the rural areas include Gonaïves, Les Cayes, and Jacmel.

Haiti's capital, Port-au-Prince, as seen from the city's harbor. The only major city in Haiti, Port-au-Prince is home to 2 million people.

Due to the relentless poverty, coupled with political insecurity and even persecution at times, some Haitians opt to leave their country altogether rather than relocate within Haiti. Some feel so desperate with their current situation that they leave in overcrowded, rickety boats, risking their lives in the hope of reaching a new, better place to call home. Since the early 1960s as many as fifty thousand Haitians have been emigrating each year. They often immigrate to the Dominican Republic, Cuba, Jamaica, the United States, and Canada.

Those who remain in Haiti—rich and poor alike—may suffer horrendous political insecurity on their small third of an island, but this common distress does not instill in them a sense of shared national identity and destiny. As observer Jennifer L. McCoy puts it, Haitians fail to see that "they are all in the same boat, and that if one group or class goes overboard, the whole boat will capsize."[11]

Even so, most Haitians grow up thinking of themselves as two separate groups that are not dependent on one another. It is this philosophy that perhaps most contributes to the continuing decline of a nation already in desperate need of cooperation. Says McCoy, "Haitian elites honestly believe, and have believed for a century and a half, that they can survive without the poor, rural majority of Haiti."[12]

FROM SLAVERY TO IN-DEPENDENT REPUBLIC: THE 1500S TO 1800S

Konstitisyon se papye, bayonèt se fè.
The constitution is made of paper, but the bayonet is
made of steel.
> —Catherine A. Sunshine and
> Deborah Menkart, eds., *Teaching About Haiti*

Haiti's early years testify to humankind's tenacious desire for freedom. Slaves under cruel and oppressive conditions defeated their masters, and even the largest expedition of Napoléon Bonaparte's forces to set sail from Europe. Without formal education or experience in self-government, the former slaves then forged a new nation. Although they endured many complex struggles and divisions along the way, Haitians can proudly claim that their country was born of one of the world's few successful slave revolts. Furthermore, Haiti became the second independent nation in the Western Hemisphere; the U.S. colonies had won their freedom from England twenty-eight years earlier.

GOLD FEVER

Christopher Columbus sighted Hispaniola on his maiden 1492 voyage to the New World. He described the island as "the most beautiful thing I have ever seen."[13] Also beautiful to the explorer's eyes were the small gold pieces with which the native Taíno people adorned themselves.

The Spaniards who followed Columbus to Hispaniola set about "Christianizing" and enslaving the Taíno to extract the island's gold. The gold was found in riverbeds, separated out by panning. But the Spaniards, convinced they could locate underground lodes, forced the Taíno to labor in unproductive mines.

21

This print depicts the cruelty with which the Spanish enslaved Native American populations.

By 1548 fewer than five hundred Taíno had survived the European invasion. Theirs was a genocide caused by over-work, disease, and outright cruelty. One Spanish priest reported that "the [conquering soldiers] would test their swords and manly strength on captured Indians and place bets on the slicing off of heads or the cutting of bodies in half with one blow."[14]

Haiti's gold was quickly as exhausted as its native people. Actually, the Spaniards soon learned there was not much of it on the island's western portion. As a result, they moved to eastern Hispaniola; the western portion, now Haiti, lapsed into neglect.

FRENCH BUCCANEERS

In the early 1600s French hunters settled on Hispaniola's abandoned northwestern coasts. Surviving Carib Indians taught them how to preserve meat by smoking it; such meat was called *buccan*. The hunters became known as buccaneers when they exchanged their cured meat for other goods from passing ships.

After England seized Jamaica—an island very close to Hispaniola—from Spain in 1655, the Spanish decided to rid the area of all foreigners, including the buccaneers. They went about the job ruthlessly. The buccaneers escaped to Tortuga Island, a naturally rocky fortress. They eventually built boats and took to the sea as pirates. The buccaneers avenged the Spaniards' cruelty by preying on ships returning to Spain loaded with gold and silver from Mexico and Peru.

Because French-speaking buccaneers were living there, France's King Louis XIV militarily claimed Tortuga and western Hispaniola in 1659. Under its first governor, Bertrand d'Ogeron, a buccaneer with a gift for managing people, the inhabitants of Tortuga and northwestern Hispaniola gradually turned from pirating to planting. Some consider d'Ogeron the true father of French Haiti, then called Saint Domingue. At one point d'Ogeron wrote, "I have had to govern fierce people who have never known any yoke and I have governed them so readily that they have attempted only two small seditions [uprisings]."[15] Eventually, the French planters spread south and west.

NEW "GOLD"

By the 1720s French colonists discovered a new form of "gold" in Saint Domingue—its rich soil. Exporting crops to Europe proved profitable, and colonists rushed in to stake out plantations. They faced a major problem, however: a desperate need for labor. To solve the dilemma, they imported African slaves. A 1791 census listed half a million slaves living in Saint Domingue. Under the burning sun, these slaves raised the crops that made the colonists wealthy. Sociologist James G. Leyburn describes the planters' lifestyle:

> Production, particularly of sugar and coffee, steadily increased until the tiny colony ranked among the wealthiest regions of the world. The Spanish Indies [Caribbean islands under Spain] were declining so that Saint-Domingue alone far outranked them all combined [in exports] between 1766 and 1791. Splendid roads were built, extensive irrigation projects developed, and stately

In the 1700s, the labor of African slaves made Haiti one of the wealthiest regions in the world.

mansions erected. Life moved along with ceremony and display—for the planters. . . . Many of these well-to-do colonials spent half their time in Paris, ostentatiously spending their riches. . . . Perhaps nowhere in the Americas was existence at once so delightful and so ornamental as it was for the wealthy planters among the 36,000 whites of Saint-Domingue in 1791.[16]

As the eighteenth century neared its end, Saint Domingue's production was vital to the French economy. The colony raised more sugar and coffee than any other place in the world. In 1789 about two-thirds of France's foreign commercial interests were centered in Saint Domingue.

CURRENTS OF DISCONTENT

Beneath the glitter, two strong currents of discontent were cresting. One came from the twenty-eight thousand mulattos and freed slaves who, since 1685, had been equal with free whites under French law. Many owned land and slaves of their own, sent their children to France for education, and participated in high society and government.

In 1734, however, the French monarchy began issuing discriminatory decrees. First, heavy penalties were imposed on whites who married mulattos. In 1767 people of mixed blood and freed slaves were barred from carrying firearms. By 1771 they could not eat at the same table with whites, were forbidden to wear European clothing fashions, and could not hold public office or pursue various occupations. They had to be off the streets by 9:00 P.M. and were seated in segregated sections in theaters and churches.

The second discontented group was the slaves. Slave treatment had reached unparalleled barbarism in Saint Domingue. Landowners desired quick profits on their investments, which sometimes meant terrorizing slaves to inspire fear in them. Researcher Carolyn E. Fick relates some methods used by Saint Domingue landowners to brutalize slaves:

A SWISS TRAVELER VISITS A SUGAR PLANTATION

In the mid-1700s a Swiss traveler named Girod-Chantrans described what he saw on a typical sugar plantation in Saint Domingue. This passage is taken from *The Making of Haiti: The Saint Domingue Revolution from Below* by Carolyn E. Fick.

The slaves numbered roughly one hundred men and women of different ages, all engaged in digging ditches in a [sugar] cane field [in preparation for planting the cane], most of them naked or dressed in rags. The sun beat straight down on their heads; sweat ran from all parts of their bodies. Their arms and legs, worn out by excessive heat, by the weight of their picks and by the resistance of the clayey soil [which had] become so hardened that it broke their tools, the slaves nevertheless made tremendous efforts to overcome all obstacles. A dead silence reigned among them. In their faces, one could see the human suffering and pain they endured, but the time for rest had not yet come. The merciless eye of the plantation steward watched over the workers while several foremen, dispersed among the workers and armed with long whips, delivered harsh blows to those who seemed too weary to sustain the pace and were forced to slow down. Men, women, young and old alike—none escaped the crack of the whip if they could not keep up the pace.

While administering the whip, they would stop, place a burning piece of wood on the slave's buttocks, and then continue, rendering the subsequent blows all the more painful. Common was the practice of pouring pepper, salt, lemon, ashes or quicklime on the slave's open and bleeding wounds. . . . Other examples exist of slaves being thrown into hot ovens and consumed by fire; of being tied to a skewer above an open fire, there to roast to death. . . . There were masters who would stuff a slave with gunpowder—like a cannon—and blow him to pieces.[17]

Such intimidation kept the slaves—who greatly outnumbered the French colonists—submissive. According to Fick, "On one level, only the sheer terrorism and brute force . . . could keep the slaves from killing [their masters] off. . . . It was through terror that the colonists instilled fear in the slaves and through fear that the slaves' labor was motivated."[18]

TAKING TO THE HILLS

Daily, slaves endured exhausting labor on a scant diet. During the sugar harvest, lasting five to six months, a slave could easily work eighteen to twenty hours daily since the mills operated nonstop. During nonharvest months, slaves worked twelve or more hours daily and ate only small amounts of beans, manioc, or boiled potatoes. In 1702 one of the wealthiest planters wrote bluntly that "Negros steal [food] at night because they are not fed by their masters."[19]

This condition continued until at least 1784, when landowners were required by law to allot slave families their own kitchen gardens. Although the gardens improved diets, they also caused the slaves to spend their little free time, Sundays and holidays, tending their gardens. Meanwhile, slave owners felt no further obligation to feed them.

Such dismal existences prompted many slaves to run away. Those who managed to escape and find refuge in the island's interior wilderness became known as Maroons. Entire Maroon settlements sprang up. From these fortified and disciplined communities—surrounded by palisades and deep ditches lined with sharpened stakes—the fugitives periodically raided plantations for food and arms, striking out at landowners in what today is considered guerrilla warfare.

SLAVERY IN SAINT DOMINGUE: SAVAGE AND SADISTIC

Slavery is never humane, but sometimes the treatment of slaves goes beyond even the inhumane. Such was the case of slavery in Saint Domingue. The atrocities reported are almost too cruel to imagine. Yet a former Saint Domingue slave named Vastey vividly describes just how depraved humans can sometimes become in their treatment of others. Vastey's description is taken from Robert Debs Heinl Jr. and Nancy Gordon Heinl's book, *Written in Blood*:

Have they not hung up men with heads downward, drowned them in sacks, crucified them on planks, buried them alive, crushed them in mortars? Have they not forced them to eat s——? And, after having flayed them with the lash, have they not cast them alive to be devoured by worms, or onto anthills, or lashed them to stakes in the swamp to be devoured by mosquitoes? Have they not thrown them into boiling caldrons of cane syrup? Have they not put men and women inside barrels studded with spikes and rolled them down mountainsides into the abyss? Have they not consigned these miserable blacks to man-eating dogs until the latter, sated by human flesh, left the mangled victims to be finished off with bayonet and poniard [a dagger]?

A group of Frenchmen prepare to punish their slaves. The French treatment of slaves in Haiti was often barbaric.

Authors Robert Debs Heinl Jr. and Nancy Gordon Heinl believe the possibility of running away and joining the Maroons "gave the slaves attainable hope of escape from bondage. It also kept alive African traditions and practices." And when engaged in skirmishes, "the slaves maintained a warrior tradition and gained proficiency in arms."[20]

Maroons relied heavily on plantation slaves, who sheltered and fed them when necessary, helped them obtain provisions, and kept them abreast of goings-on among the landowners. Similarly, freed blacks also frequently took risks to harbor and help fugitives slaves even though French law stipulated that, for assisting runaways, freed blacks would be resold into slavery along with their families.

"LOADED BARRELS OF GUNPOWDER"

A surge in slaves escaping to Maroon communities, along with more daring Maroon guerrilla activity during the 1770s, led many observers to believe that some kind of change was coming. The atmosphere became so tense that, in 1783, the marquis du Rouvray, an elderly planter and colonial army officer, wrote, "This colony of slaves is like a city under the imminence of attack; we are treading on loaded barrels of gunpowder."[21]

Du Rouvray was right. The fuse was lit in 1791 at a religious ceremony attended by delegates from more than one hundred of Saint Domingue's northern plantations. Researcher Davis describes the event:

> The historic gathering was invoked by the Maroon leader Boukman Dutty, and held on a secluded knoll at Bois Caiman [Alligator Woods]. There on August 14, 1791, beneath the spindly branches of a frail acacia, with the wind twisting the ground and the jagged lightning crashing on all sides, an old woman stood transfixed by the night, quivering in the spasms of possession [of spirits, who through her voice called for rebellion]. . . . The leaders were named [Boukman and three others] and one by one the hundreds of slaves swore allegiance.[22]

RAINING FIRE

Within days dozens of northern plantations were torched, their white inhabitants were killed, and their sugar and coffee mills were destroyed. Says Davis, "For days dark columns of smoke rose beyond a wall of flames that isolated the entire northern half of the colony. Fire rained from the clouds of burning straw torn from fields and swept by the fireballs. Ash coated the sea, and the image of an entire land aflame reddened clouds as far away as the Bahamas."[23]

Two months of warfare ensued. By November the northern landowners had been defeated and their plantations were in ruins. Colonists escaped to the coastal city of Cap Français and crammed into ships to return to France. Despite their victory, the rebels lost their leader, Boukman, who was captured and beheaded.

TOUSSAINT-LOUVERTURE EMERGES

François-Dominique Toussaint-Louverture emerged as the first leader of Saint Domingue's black masses. He was born in the early 1740s on the Breda estate, whose owner treated slaves compassionately. A freed slave on the plantation taught Toussaint-Louverture to read and write French.

Toussaint-Louverture rose to the position of coachman to the plantation manager, Bayon de Libertas. Just a week or two before the August 14, 1791, declaration of revolution, Libertas personally asked Touissant-Louverture to keep order on the plantation and to protect his wife while he was away on business. Touissant-Louverture gave his word, although he had no idea that neighboring plantations would soon be burning or that the thousand Breda slaves would be eager to join the revolution. Knowing he could not keep peace on the estate for long, Touissant-Louverture helped Madame de Libertas get safely to Cap Français.

Led by Toussaint-Louverture, Haitian slaves were successful in driving out their French masters.

TOUSSAINT-LOUVERTURE: PHYSICIAN TO A NATION

François-Dominique Toussaint-Louverture was born in 1743 or 1744 on the Breda plantation in northern Saint Domingue. His mother was a slave; the identity of his father is unclear. However, a black freedman named Pierre Baptiste, who had attended a Jesuit school, exerted much influence on the boy. Baptiste taught Toussaint-Louverture to read and write French. An eager student, Toussaint-Louverture spent his free time learning.

Baptiste also taught Toussaint-Louverture the medicinal properties of plants and herbs. Toussaint-Louverture used this knowledge to heal, earning the nickname "the Physician" among Breda's slaves.

As a child, Touissant-Louverture became a stable helper. He learned to ride exceptionally well—a skill that served him later as a military commander. He eventually became the plantation manager's coachman, a position that provided freedom of movement and the chance to network with other estates. He eventually married a woman named Suzanne; they had two sons and a happy relationship.

Although his own life was not unduly harsh—his master insisted that the Breda slaves be treated well—Toussaint-Louverture remained deeply moved by the plight of his fellow slaves. Shortly after revolt broke out in 1791, he joined the rebel forces and shone as a brilliant military strategist. Some say he received the last name Louverture, meaning "Opening," due to an uncanny ability to find critical openings during battles.

Toussaint-Louverture channeled this energy to fight for freedom for Saint Domingue's slaves—without harboring bitterness toward whites. Unfortunately, his career was cut short when he was captured, taken to France, and was thrown into a cold dungeon, where he died of pneumonia on April 7, 1803.

Toussaint-Louverture

Once Madame de Libertas was secure and his own wife, Suzanne, and their two sons had crossed the border into Spanish Hispaniola, Toussaint-Louverture and the Breda slaves joined the revolutionary forces. At first, the two remaining rebel leaders, Georges Biassou and Jean-François, were suspicious of Toussaint-Louverture. After all, he had assisted whites and had tarried in joining the rebels. Toussaint-Louverture, however, soon convinced Biassou and Jean-François of his sincerity and devotion to ending slavery. Literate in French, he served as Biassou's military secretary. Toussaint-Louverture was also placed in charge of troops, where his genius for military strategy quickly flowered.

EUROPEAN POWERS AT WAR

The next decade evolved into a confusing mishmash of shifting alliances between Saint Domingue's rebel leaders and the European powers—France, Spain, and England. The French Revolution (1789–1799) caused Haiti's rebel leaders to interact with two French factions during these ten years— those still loyal to the monarchy and the French revolutionaries who had assumed power. Furthermore, France and England were enemies during this time, declaring outright war in 1793. And the Spanish, controlling what is now the Dominican Republic, would have relished retaking Saint Domingue from the French.

The French were the first to go. On June 21, 1793, amid squabbles between the two French factions in Cap Français, French revolutionary leaders called in fifteen thousand slaves and instructed them to wreck havoc on the city. The city's white inhabitants quickly boarded the ships in harbor. As they departed, they could see Cap Français being torched. "The flames that consumed [the city] signaled the end of white supremacy and slavery in Saint Domingue,"[24] note historians Heinl and Heinl. Slavery had not yet been officially abolished by the French government, however, which still held Haiti as a colony.

FIGHTING SPANISH AND ENGLISH TROOPS

Both the Spanish and English sent troops into Saint Domingue. The British won much of the southern part of the colony and restored slavery in their territory, including Port-au-Prince. Both countries hoped to take advantage of

France's internal divisions and weakened state by plucking this Caribbean pearl, capable of producing so much wealth and strategically located alongside the Windward Passage (an important sea route), for themselves.

However, by 1794 Toussaint-Louverture was leading an entire army and actively fought the British for four years, until their surrender. And by 1801, Toussaint-Louverture had become supreme commander of the entire island of Hispaniola—having also conquered the Spanish territory—and put an end to slavery.

The slaves had successfully rid themselves of their tyrannical French masters and had driven off the British and Spaniards who would re-enslave them. Yet there was still a problem. Saint Domingue remained a French colony, and, technically, slavery was still a legal institution. Although French rulers claimed slavery had been abolished, Toussaint-Louverture and others were not sure whether it truly had been, and if so, whether it could be easily reinstated by decree.

NAPOLÉON'S IRRITATION

At the beginning of the nineteenth century, Toussaint-Louverture and his country of former slaves faced that problem head on. Although Toussaint-Louverture knew Hispaniola was still a French colony, he ruled as if it were independent. He had written a constitution providing for local self-government and a leader to be elected for life. He would be that leader.

Toussaint-Louverture's proclamation was ill timed, however. In October 1801 France's war with England ended, lifting the British naval blockade in the Caribbean and giving France freedom on the seas. Napoléon Bonaparte, who had taken control of France in 1799, had been waiting for just such an opportunity to turn his attention to the West Indies; despite the slaves' efforts, he had no intention of losing France's wealthiest colony. He also intended to establish a western empire spreading out from Louisiana (in what is now the southern United States), using Saint Domingue as a base of operations. He was further angered that Toussaint-Louverture had named himself ruler of a colony Napoléon considered his own.

"Napoleon was irritated beyond measure at the effrontery of Toussaint's seizure of power in the colony,"[25] writes Leyburn. By December 1801 Napoléon had 21,175 soldiers and an armada of sixty-seven ships sailing the Atlantic.

FENDING OFF THE FRENCH—AGAIN!

Napoléon chose General Charles-Victor-Emmanuel Leclerc, his brother-in-law, to head the operation. In written instructions to Leclerc, Napoléon laid out his plan for asserting control over Saint Domingue and reinstating slavery. He wrote,

> Ship out all black generals, regardless of their conduct, patriotism, or past services. . . . No matter what happens, disarm all *noirs* [blacks], whatever their party, and put them to work. . . . Whites who have served Toussaint will be [deported] . . . White women who have prostituted themselves to *noirs*, whatever their rank, will be deported to Europe.[26]

Publicly, however, and in a letter to Toussaint-Louverture, Napoléon claimed he wanted freedom for blacks. Toussaint-Louverture was not fooled. Instead, he formulated a plan of his own. "Toussaint's strategy [was] simple and ruthless," comment the Heinls. "It would be to burn the towns, lay waste the habitations, kill the *blancs* [whites], fall back into the *mornes* [mountains], wait for the climate to cripple the French, and massacre the survivors."[27]

Henri Christophe—Touissant-Louverture's black general in charge of Cap Français—was the first to use this tactic. When Leclerc made moves to enter the city on February 4, 1802, Christophe ordered the citizens to evacuate. Christophe then torched first his own mansion and then the elegant city, and he then retreated to the hills with his troops. Leclerc ultimately landed on a city reduced to ashes.

Wanting to use Haiti as a base of operations, Napoléon sent an army to reconquer the region.

CUTTING ONLY THE TRUNK

The French had disembarked at many other points as well, and they had convinced southern leaders that they had come merely to protect the colony and to preserve peace. Haiti's leaders in the north and west were not so easily persuaded, though, and they engaged the French in intense battles, with many deaths. By April, despite their courageous resistance, both Christophe and Toussaint-Louverture, over-powered by the French troops and their firepower, were secretly negotiating a truce with the French.

The two did surrender, but Leclerc felt uneasy about them, particularly about Toussaint-Louverture. On June 6, 1802, Leclerc wrote to a government minister in Paris, "Toussaint is not to be trusted. . . . I am going to order his arrest. . . . As soon as I have him safe, I shall ship him off to Corsica [a French island] for imprisonment."[28]

When Toussaint-Louverture arrived for a meeting with one of Leclerc's officers the following day, soldiers bundled him off to a waiting ship. Despite his capture, Toussaint-Louverture was still certain the rebellion would succeed because he knew just how intensely Haiti's blacks detested slavery. To the ship's captain, Toussaint-Louverture said, "In overthrowing me they have cut off only the trunk of the tree of black liberty. It will flourish again through its roots. They are many and deep."[29] Toussaint-Louverture died of pneumonia less than a year later in a cold prison in the Alps.

Toussaint-Louverture's surrender and capture brought peace to Saint Domingue, but not for long. The martyred leader's words came true when news spread throughout Haiti that Napoléon had restored slavery on nearby Guadeloupe and that he had resumed the slave trade. These two events proved to be the incentive the slaves needed to wrestle the colony from France forever.

LIBERTY OR DEATH

Many former slaves did not mind remaining subjects of France, but none wanted to be reshackled. They quickly realized, though, that remaining under the control of France meant returning to slavery. By the time Leclerc tried to disarm them, the masses knew they had to rid their island of the French completely or be returned to the plantations. Huge Maroon bands soon re-formed and spread, engaging the French in skirmishes throughout the colony using mostly guerrilla warfare.

Says Carolyn E. Fick, "The whole burden of resistance now lay squarely on [the black masses'] shoulders, and for resisting they would face firing squads, be hanged, drowned, even gassed to death. The reprisals were terrible, and yet such atrocities seemed only to reinforce [their] determination."[30]

Haitians continued to fight for their liberty even after Toussaint-Louverture (shown here) died in prison.

These people were willing to risk everything to secure their freedom. According to Fick,

One woman, reportedly, had turned to her husband who seemed hesitant as they were both about to die, and said: "Do you not know how sublime it is to die for liberty?" whereupon she proudly took hold of the rope and hung herself rather than die at the hands of the hangman. Another woman . . . consoled her weeping daughters, who marched with her toward the place of execution: "Rejoice that your wombs will not have to bear slave children."[31]

Resistance grew so widespread that Toussaint-Louverture's black generals—who had surrendered to the French—now defected back to the masses. Christophe and Jean-Jacques Dessalines, born a slave to a vicious master, teamed up with mulatto general Alexandre Pétion to help defeat the French.

In addition to the Haitians' dogged insurgency, a disease called yellow fever also played a role in defeating the French. When spring rains began, the island's coasts teemed with mosquitoes carrying the yellow fever virus. Although Haiti's black masses had built immunity to the disease, the Europeans had not. By August, in one hospital alone, a hundred European soldiers were dying daily. By the end of October 1802, yellow fever claimed General Leclerc himself.

By November 1803 the French capitulated. The former slaves of Saint Domingue had won their freedom.

INDEPENDENCE

On January 1, 1804, Dessalines proclaimed independence and declared himself leader, choosing the indigenous Taíno

Dogged by the Haitians' determination and decimated by yellow fever, the French army was unable to take possession of Haiti.

name Ayiti meaning "Mountainous," for the new republic. Dessalines, however, proved to be a tyrant who ruled by intimidation and threats. Facing a country in ruins and fearing possible attacks by the French at any moment, Dessalines felt he needed an iron grip on his citizens.

To impose order and control, Dessalines decreed that all citizens must be either soldiers or laborers on plantations. In effect, Dessalines re-created the old arrangement of forced labor, even though the workers were serfs rather than slaves and most land belonged to the state rather than to individuals. Under this system, the fields again yielded abundant harvests, and sugar refineries were rebuilt.

THE NEW NATION IS DIVIDED

When political foes assassinated Dessalines in October 1806, southern and northern Haitians could not agree on his successor. A brief civil war ensued, with neither side emerging victorious. For the next twenty years, the tiny new republic remained divided. General Henri Christophe ruled in the north, where he built a colossal fortress and had himself crowned Emperor Henry I. General Pétion and then Jean-Pierre Boyer ruled in the south.

Jean-Pierre Boyer wanted color distinctions abolished.

When Christophe died in 1820, Boyer reunited the north and south peacefully, becoming the ruler of all of Haiti. During his thirteen-year reign, class distinctions based on skin color began to re-form. This was not Boyer's intention, though. In fact, he felt Haiti's future lay in abolishing color distinctions and prejudices. However, the country's education system inadvertently ensured that the wealthy mulattos (who generally had more access to education) rose higher and more often in the government than the country's uneducated, poor blacks. Since governmental posts required literacy, most positions went to young mulatto men. Ambitious black youth tended to choose army careers, where literacy was not needed for promotion. This initiated a trend that would become a deeply rooted practice—Haiti's civil government run by mulattos and its military controlled by blacks.

INTRIGUES AND INSURRECTIONS

Antagonism between mulattos and blacks grew during the next seventy years, a fact that was reflected in the country's political turmoil. From the end of Boyer's presidency in 1843 until 1915, Haiti had twenty-two heads of state. Of these, only one served his full term. Six died in office, one resigned, and fourteen others were deposed by revolutions or coups. One observer succinctly put it this way: "The history of the country . . . is but a series of plots and revolutions followed by barbarous military executions."[32]

The rural peasants, however, the great majority of Haitians, were mostly removed from the political chaos of the cities. By the start of the twentieth century, the peasants had experienced some seventy-five years of farming in relative peace. The struggle had been long and bloody, but Haiti's former slaves had overcome tremendous odds to overthrow mighty and tyrannical forces. Their sons and daughters now held a degree of control over their own destinies.

MODERN HAITI'S UNSETTLED POLITICAL ORDER

Ròch nan dlo pa konnen mizè ròch nan solèy.
Rocks in the water don't know the misery of rocks in
the sun.
— Edner A. Jeanty and O. Carl Brown,
Parol Granmoun: Haitian Popular Wisdom

Haiti remained isolated throughout the 1800s. Some world powers even shunned the country to avoid Haitian independence influencing their own slaves. During the 1900s, though, that policy ended. In an attempt to establish itself as the sole power in the Western Hemisphere and out of fear that the Germans (during World War I) would establish a military base in the Caribbean, the United States forced Haiti out of isolation. This foreign intervention, however, did not stabilize Haiti or help Haitians build their own institutions. Rather, it reinforced patterns that encouraged Haiti to continue on a chaotic political course.

PREVENTING GERMAN INFLUENCE

At the beginning of the twentieth century, Germans became active in Haitian society and business. They married Haitians, skirting the Haitian prohibition against foreigners owning land. They established communities, and couples sent their German-Haitian children to Germany for schooling. According to historians, "German merchants . . . assimilated with Haitians and their society more successfully than any other foreign group."[33]

The United States was unhappy with this trend, particularly when Germans purchased key Haitian industries, including a railroad and several electric companies. With construction of the Panama Canal, the United States wanted, for military security, to control the Caribbean. So in 1913, the United States decided to intervene in Haiti. Historian Hans Schmidt explains:

While the decision to intervene in Haiti was part of the long-term development of the United States hegemony [control] in the Caribbean, the threat of German incursion was a more immediate factor and ultimately the decisive one. State Department tactics for executing the intervention evolved over two years, beginning with diplomatic efforts . . . and ending with the landing of Marines.[34]

THE CATALYST

The Americans had to wait, though, for a precipitating political event, something that would give the U.S. military just cause to go into Haiti. That event came two years later when a man named Vilbrun Guillaume Sam gathered together a band of Cacos, or peasant mercenary soldiers, in northern Haiti. The Cacos captured a northern town and proceeded to Port-au-Prince, where they ensured Sam's election as president.

President Sam did not last long. After assuming power, he immediately seized hostages—some two hundred boys and young men from mulatto families—and imprisoned them. This tactic, an attempt to keep members of the mulatto elite in check by holding their loved ones hostage, had been used by black leaders in the past but proved unsuccessful for Sam. Furthermore, the attention he paid the elite kept him from seeing that the biggest threat to his power was another presidential hopeful (named Dr. Rosalvo Bobo) and his own Caco band.

On July 27, 1915, Bobo and his band besieged the presidential palace in Port-au-Prince in an attempt to oust Sam from power. As the insurgents advanced, Sam realized he would not survive the assault, and he instructed his chief of police, General Charles-Oscar Etienne to do with the mulatto prisoners whatever he thought was best. Etienne, in turn, ordered a massacre of the hostages. "My comrades were slaughtered, disemboweled, dismembered, reduced to a mass of flesh,"[35] a survivor wrote. It was an action that incited riots in the streets. In retaliation, relatives of the murder victims dragged Etienne and President Sam into the street, where mobs hacked them to pieces.

THE YANKS ARE COMING

This savage lawlessness gave the United States the reason it needed to send marines to occupy Haiti. Landing on July 28, 1915, they ended up staying nineteen years.

During this period the United States counted among its major objectives controlling Haiti's finances and its bank (previously dominated by France), ridding Haiti of German influence, and establishing a Haitian police force under U.S. command. One objective missing from the list was promoting democracy. Instead of vowing to set up a democratic system in Haiti, the United States ruled the island nation militarily, encouraging the long-standing Haitian idea that the strongest force (whether the United States, the mulatto elite, or the military) would reign supreme.

The Americans' first order of business was to install a president hand-selected by leaders of the occupation. The first two presidents were Sudre Dartiguenave and Louis Borno, but they were virtually powerless politicians. They simply represented and carried out the goals of the U.S. government.

Two years later, when the legislature refused to accept a new U.S.-written constitution, occupation forces dissolved

U.S. Marines unload supplies and equipment as they arrive in Haiti.

Haiti's National Assembly. This action attacked the core of Haiti's economic system because it permitted foreign landownership, which, in turn, opened the door to American business. Since independence, Haiti's own constitutions had stood firm on one point—no foreign landownership. But the U.S. forces made it clear that Haitians and their constitutions were no longer in control of the country.

REINFORCING STRONG-ARM POLITICS

Leaders of the U.S. occupation knew that, to consolidate their power, they had to subdue the various Caco bands throughout Haiti, many of which were still loyal to Bobo. Although poorly armed (they used only old rifles and machetes), the Cacos were highly mobile. They knew Haiti's terrain and by simply hiding their weapons and removing red identifying patches from their clothing, they resembled other peasants.

Caco bands caused a lot of trouble for the Americans. They interfered with food transport into U.S.-held cities and raided marine camps. U.S. officials, in turn, eliminated Caco opposition by one of two methods—paying them to turn in their weapons or by hunting and killing them. Most often, the marines took no prisoners, and the number of Haitians killed so alarmed the secretary of the navy that in November 1915 he instructed the commanding officer, "In view of heavy losses to Haitians in recent engagement, department [the U.S. Navy] desires your offensive to be suspended in order to prevent further loss of life."[36]

Sudre Dartiguenave, a powerless politician installed by the U.S. military.

THE CORVÉE

The Americans also employed authoritarian tactics to achieve their goal of constructing roads throughout Haiti. They required Haitians to build the roads, unpaid. This system, called the corvée system, became highly unpopular because the marines trained a Haitian police force to be in charge of the laborers. The police, though, often mistreated the workers, sometimes hitting them, sometimes tying them together.

"The roping together of workers," says researcher Schmidt, "was especially upsetting to the peasants, since it recalled legends of French colonial slave gangs."[37] Hostility to the corvée became so intense that by late 1918, the United States changed its policy and paid Haitians to complete the roads.

RENEWED CACO RESISTANCE

One disobedient marine commander, however, continued to used force labor in Haiti's mountainous north-central region,

CHARLEMAGNE PÉRALTE IS IMMORTALIZED

Haitians venerate Charlemagne Péralte as a martyred hero. Intelligent, ambitious, and well educated, Péralte was outraged, as were many Haitians, over the road-building corvée imposed in 1916 by the U.S. occupation. Many Haitians believed it was a step toward their reenslavement.

From April through September 1919, U.S. Marines engaged in some 130 hostile encounters with Péralte's forces. The marines concluded that they could not squelch the rebellion until they got rid of Péralte. In *Written in Blood*, Robert Debs Heinl Jr. and Nancy Gordon Heinl quote the officer who ordered Péralte's assassination.

> It was a pretty big order. It meant running down one Haitian out of several millions in a country as big as the State of New York. And that one Haitian was surrounded by his friends, operating in a country almost entirely sympathetic to him, was protected by a fanatical bodyguard, never slept two nights in the same place, and must be run down in a tangled maze of mountains and valleys, of which there were no accurate maps.

Two marines eventually located Péralte and shot him on the spot. To convince Haitians that Péralte was indeed dead, the marines laid his almost naked body on a door, posed next to a flag, and photographed it.

Some thirty years later, renowned Haitian artist Philomé Obin used that photo to recreate the scene in the painting *Crucifixion of Charlemagne Péralte in the Name of Liberty*. Obin's image of Peralte's body—with clear echoes of the crucifixion of a suffering Christ—reverberates in the hearts of Haitians, a symbol of their lasting quest for liberty. Now in the Musée d'Art Haïtien, the painting is considered Obin's masterpiece.

where Caco activity was traditionally heaviest. Most observers confirmed the atrocities in this area, and an investigating officer, Colonel Hooker, went so far as to call the corvée there a "reign of terror."[38]

These abuses induced a young patriot, Charlemagne Péralte, to rally together several thousand band members, who vowed "to drive the invaders into the sea and free Haiti."[39] Between September 1918 and March 1919, Péralte's Cacos struck at military posts throughout the country. The marines brought in reinforcements, though, and during the next six months the two sides fought 131 engagements.

In the end, the Cacos were defeated. A U.S. marine killed Péralte on October 31, 1919, but the slain leader would become a national hero, a symbol of Haitian resistance.

As before, the marines took no prisoners, executing Cacos and even peasants merely suspected of being Cacos. It was a massacre that caught the attention of many, including one U.S. officer who, in October 1919, censured the marines, noting that "troops in the field have declared and carried on what is commonly known as 'open season,' where care is not taken to determine whether or not the natives encountered are bandits [the marine term for Cacos] or 'good citizens.'"[40]

U.S. RACIAL ATTITUDES

The U.S. occupation and the brutality it brought deeply offended Haitian pride. After 111 years of independence, Haitians of all skin hues again saw themselves governed by white men, this time from a country practicing racial segregation. The marines brought America's racist attitude to Haiti. Some were outright cruel but most simply viewed the black and mulatto Haitians as inferior. "The American Marines practiced social racism," says journalist Amy Wilentz. "They kept to themselves and thought that Haitians, even those with degrees from the Sorbonne [a prestigious French university], were not good enough to come in their front doors."[41]

U.S. WITHDRAWAL

These racial prejudices partly led to the marines' hasty departure in 1934, two years before their appointed time. Because they believed the Haitians were less intelligent and incapable of intellectual pursuits, occupation officials

U.S. Marines battle Caco rebels in the Haitian jungle.

thought they should learn manual skills. The result was the Service Technique, a program to train teachers in agriculture and technical vocations.

Begun in 1924, the Service Technique drew its students—future teachers—from the elite by offering handsome scholarships. The program was not successful and lasted only five years because the students detested having to perform manual labor. Additionally, they saw many of the service's initiatives ending in failure due to poor planning and a misunderstanding of Haitian culture.

In October 1929 the Service Technique students went on strike. Sympathy strikes among students in other schools followed. By early December Haitian politicians and businesspeople were siding with the strikers. In the wake of the demonstrations and a small skirmish in the town of Les Cayes, U.S. officials decided to leave Haiti for good, although it would take nearly five years for them to withdraw completely. Due to the nature of the occupation (basically, it was a military dictatorship), it took that amount of time to train the Haitians to govern themselves.

Haitian police patrol a street in the 1940s. After the U.S. occupation, the Haitian government continued to rule the country with military force.

Feelings were running so high that many feared the actual withdrawal could become nasty. In an attempt to thwart violence, U.S. president Franklin D. Roosevelt visited Haiti in July 1934. According to one historian, "Roosevelt's visit, and his speech, which was partly in French, created a highly favorable impression in Haiti. It was the first time in Haitian history that the chief of a foreign state had visited the country. Roosevelt's personal graciousness continued to warm Haitian-American relations in subsequent years."[42]

THE AFTERMATH

Despite the tranquil farewell, the nineteen-year U.S. occupation was, by no means, successful. Through its martial-law rule, the United States reinforced Haiti's pattern of military dictatorship and taught the Haitians nothing of democracy. In fact, U.S. officials left Haiti's government even more fragile than it had been before the occupation by their failure to train Haitians from the outset to replace them. And their last-minute efforts to train Haitians before the withdrawal proved to be too little, too late.

The Americans left in their wake a nation wrought with problems. Haiti's small inheritance of an infrastructure—clinics, roads, and ports—decayed rapidly. Only three decades later, the head of the U.S. military mission to Haiti reported, "Telephones are gone. Roads [which had never been paved] are approaching non-existence. . . . Ports are obstructed by silt and wrecks, their docks crumbling away. Urban improvements are in decay and collapse; sanitation and electrification are, to say the least, in precarious decline."[43]

Additionally, Haiti's social system (primarily health and education) was in ruins, and the nation's fierce nationalism (encouraged by U.S. racial attitudes) prevented the country from making a smooth transition to an independent nation. In the long run, the Americans did more harm than good, and Haiti's future seemed as grim (if not more so) as it had before the United States got involved.

AFTER THE U.S. DEPARTURE (1934–1957)

The two decades following the U.S. occupation proved to be one of Haiti's most settled political eras and would later be seen as a lull between two storms. Of the presidents elected during this period, only one would have special historic significance. That president was Dumarsais Estimé, elected in 1945. Estimé provided educational and civil service opportunities for black Haitians, including those of the emerging middle class. He also encouraged the career of François Duvalier, a country doctor. Estimé appointed Duvalier his minister of labor and public health, and the country doctor would soon become a leading figure in Haitian politics.

Well into the 1950s, Haitians continued to enjoy a rare period of relative economic prosperity. Both tourism and coffee boomed. "Times were good, and levels of life, both in the countryside and in the capital, were probably as high as they had been at any time in Haitian history,"[44] writes one observer. Haitians could hardly have known this interim of relative peace and prosperity would soon come to a horrific end.

FRANÇOIS DUVALIER

Duvalier and rival Louis Dejoie emerged as favorites in Haiti's 1957 presidential elections. Dejoie, a light-skinned member of the elite, was popular in the south, where he ran a large business. Duvalier, by contrast, had struggled economically to get an education and become a doctor. He enjoyed working-class support, and he championed a movement called Négritude, meaning black pride, that looked to Africa, rather than Europe, for Haitian identity.

On September 22, 1957, Haitians voted Duvalier into a six-year presidential term, and his supporters won a majority of legislative seats. Duvalier seemed to be just what Haiti needed—solemn and mild mannered. Biographer Elizabeth Abbott describes the fifty-year-old doctor as "impeccably neat, and primly dressed in dark suits and hats in winter and white suits and hats in summer. He appeared everywhere with his wife, Simone, at his side, her frail innocence and schoolmarm dresses as disarming as his own grave respectability."[45]

This persona proved to be untrue, however. In fact, Duvalier was much more vicious than calm. He harbored a hatred of both the army and the elite, who he believed oppressed the black masses. Duvalier had also studied the writings of Machiavelli, a sixteenth-century philosopher who advocated using any means necessary (no matter how unethical) to obtain political power.

Almost as soon as inaugural ceremonies were completed on October 22, 1957, Duvalier demonstrated that he, as Machiavelli had proposed, would use any method, however ruthless, to suppress real or imagined enemies. Says historian Abbott,

François "Papa Doc" Duvalier ruled Haiti with an iron fist.

From his first days in the cursed presidential chair, Duvalier tirelessly eliminated his opponents. Before he could begin to implement policy, he explained to his intimates, he had to ensure his own power. With vicious Clément Barbot in charge of his secret police, and hooded men . . . as his armed goons, Duvalier instituted the sneak arrests and brutal interrogations often followed by death or permanent disappearance that were to mark his regime.[46]

In March 1958 Duvalier took over the Haitian military. But still not trusting the military, he also fashioned his own security organization, the National Security Volunteers, which Haitians dubbed "Tonton Macoutes." (In Haitian folklore, the tonton macoute is the fairy-tale bogeyman who whisks away naughty children in his large sack.) In the cities, Tonton Macoutes were recruited from the shantytowns; in the rural areas, they were often Vodun leaders.

"I HAVE MASTERED THE COUNTRY"

Within two years Duvalier's Macoutes had imprisoned, banished, or murdered most present and potential opponents. Duvalier justified his tyrannical behavior by claiming that God had chosen him to rule Haiti. On August 5, 1958, he issued such a proclamation to the nation: "I have mastered the country. I have mastered power. I am the New Haiti. To seek to destroy me is to seek to destroy Haiti herself. . . . No earthly power can prevent me from accomplishing my historic mission because it is God and Destiny who have chosen me."[47]

Duvalier only got worse with time, and following a massive heart attack in May 1959, close associates felt the dictator had

A group of François Duvalier's "Tonton Macoutes" march in front of the presidential palace.

HOW DUVALIER CAME TO BE "PAPA DOC"

This excerpt relates the work of then thirty-six-year-old
François Duvalier—some fourteen years before he was elected
president of Haiti—and explains how he earned the nickname
"Papa Doc." It is taken from *HAITI: The Duvaliers and Their
Legacy* by Elizabeth Abbott.

In 1943, Duvalier's life changed. The U.S. changed it. The
Inter-American Affairs Commission sent Dr. James
Dwinelle to Haiti to direct a massive medical campaign
[using penicillin] against yaws, the crippling tropical disease affecting three-quarters of all Haitians. Highly con-
tagious, yaws enters the body in the form of a spirochete
[spiral-shaped bacteria] through the bare soles [of the
feet]. Left untreated, it eats away at its victims. Their limbs
wither and deform, they suffer great purulent ulcerations
[pus-filled sores] all over their bodies, and they lose their
noses and lips just as lepers do. Also like lepers, they were
often driven off with stones by unafflicted neighbors.

Dr. Dwinelle . . . hired [Duvalier] to direct the Rural Clinic
of Gressier, fifteen miles southwest of Port-au-Prince, the
most yaws-ridden area of Haiti. . . . The anti-yaws campaign orchestrated through the Gressier clinic finally succeeded in ridding Haiti of the dread disease, and in
transforming the shy scholarly myopic [near-sighted] little Duvalier into the great country doctor who cured hundreds of thousands, and whose reputation as their "Papa
Doc" spread as steadily as yaws contracted. By June over
one thousand daily rode their mules down mountain
tracks or hobbled on decaying feet along dusty village
paths to the clinic where they were finally cured.

lapsed into madness. Says Abbott, "Without killing Duvalier,
[the heart attack] transformed him into a man who lacked
mental balance, a dictator who . . . would suddenly rant and
rave and foam at the mouth like a true lunatic, astonishing
and horrifying onlookers."[48]

Duvalier's lunacy was marked by paranoia. In April 1963
his former right-hand man, Barbot, shot to death a chauffeur
and three bodyguards as they left two of the four Duvalier
children at school. Not knowing who had carried out the as-

sassinations, Duvalier suspected everyone. "From then on no child was safe in Haiti, no mother or grandmother, for at any moment Duvalier might take them as hostages to punish those he suspected of plotting against him,"[49] writes Abbott.

Duvalier's actions did not go unnoticed. In 1967 the International Commission of Jurists, based in Switzerland and dedicated to peace through law, denounced Duvalier's policies and reported this about Haiti:

> The systematic violation of every single article and paragraph of the Universal Declaration of Human Rights seems to be the only policy which is respected and assiduously pursued in this Caribbean Republic. The rule of law was long ago displaced by a reign of terror and the personal will of its dictator. . . . He is leading his nation . . . towards the final disaster that can be seen in its political, social, and economic collapse.[50]

The shy doctor who had, as a young man, endeared himself to so many peasants, had become a butcher. During his fourteen-year dictatorship Duvalier—indirectly through his Tonton Macoutes and sometimes directly—presided over the deaths of an estimated thirty to sixty thousand Haitians.

Baby Doc

In January 1971, three months before he died, Duvalier proclaimed his only son, Jean-Claude Duvalier, as his successor. The two became known as "Papa Doc" and "Baby Doc." Jean-Claude, then nineteen years old, governed with the help of his mother, Simone Ovide Duvalier.

Unlike his father, Jean-Claude had no interest in politics. His interests centered on partying, racing cars and motorcycles, hunting, and sports. Although his grade school classmates had teased him, Jean-Claude grew into a man who was pleasant and made friends easily. Whereas his father had been a workaholic, Baby Doc desired only to enjoy life.

As the years passed, though, Jean-Claude Duvalier's lifestyle required more and more money, and the young president discovered a way to keep cash flowing into his accounts. By creating the impression that Haiti was again law-abiding and caring about its citizens, Baby Doc obtained funds from countries and organizations concerned about

Jean-Claude "Baby Doc" Duvalier and his wife, Michèle. Although not as cruel as his father, Baby Doc and Michèle misused public funds for personal gain.

the suffering of Haiti's masses. He then used portions of that money to support his lavish lifestyle.

His wife also plundered public funds for personal gain. Michèle Bennett, whom Jean-Claude married in 1980, was the daughter of a wealthy mulatto family. Her spending habits became scandalous and shocked most Haitians. She paid fifty thousand dollars a month, for example, to have fresh flowers flown in from Florida to decorate the presidential palace.

It was general knowledge in Haiti that politicians used public funds for personal gain. But Bennett carried it too far. Comments journalist Amy Wilentz,

What was unacceptable was her ostentation: the wedding reception, the ranch, the mountain retreat, the beachfront mansion, the alleged cocaine abuse, the million-dollar decorating binges, the million-dollar shopping trips to Paris and New York, the furs. Haitians in general were disgusted, and the black middle class and the rest of the mulatto elite were jealous.[51]

ANTI-DUVALIER PROTESTS

Although Baby Doc was not as cruel as his father, his regime was not without terror. In May 1984 police officers beat to death a pregnant woman. This barbarism sent thousands into the street protesting the government.

Protests, both organized and spontaneous, continued throughout the country over the next year. In November 1985 schoolchildren and young people in Gonaïves peacefully demonstrated, later joined by anti-Duvalier throngs. The next day Macoutes ran down and killed three schoolboys, blaming the schoolchildren for sparking the unrest. Rioting spread further.

OUSTING THE PRESIDENT

Meanwhile, one of Baby Doc's cabinet members, who had witnessed the mobs in Gonaïves, came to believe that Duvalier should be removed from office and exiled. He consulted a few army officers, who agreed. U.S. officials in Haiti also agreed with the army officers that Baby Doc should go, even though the United States had long supported Duvalier's government because it was solidly anti-Communist.

The group members planning the Duvaliers' ouster knew they needed to obtain at least the neutrality of top Macoutes if they were to get the Duvaliers out of Haiti without a bloodbath. Once the Macoute leaders learned the U.S. government no longer backed Baby Doc, they agreed not to interfere as he was removed from office. On February 7, 1986, Jean-Claude Duvalier, his wife, and extended family agreed to be exiled to Paris.

The group that removed Baby Doc from office was unique because, as one analyst says,

it was not an armed insurgency. Nor was it a movement led by politicians. Rather, the driving energy came from

Haitian youth, especially in the provincial towns and rural areas. Their efforts were encouraged by a grassroots religious movement whose principal impetus came from new forces within the Catholic Church. Radio stations, broadcasting in Creole [Kreyòl], became critical sources of information for a population which was 80 percent illiterate.[52]

Despite the fact that the Duvaliers were no longer in power, Haiti's masses still did not see a stable government installed, nor were their dire needs for food, housing, education, and medical services met. The years of vicious and self-serving dictators would prove virtually impossible to overcome.

PROBLEMS AFTER DUVALIER

Part of the problem was that those organizing the Duvaliers' farewell had given little thought to what would happen next. U.S. officials asked for an interim government of both civilians and military officers until elections could be held. General Henri Namphy, Haiti's army commander and a key

Haitians dance and cheer in the streets of Port-au-Prince to celebrate the exile of Jean-Claude Duvalier.

player in getting the Duvaliers out, was named president of the provisional government.

Another enormous problem was what to do with the armed Tonton Macoutes roaming Haiti. The new government officially disbanded the Macoutes and took many to army barracks under armed guard. Citizens wanted the Macoutes tried for their crimes, however, and they became suspicious when a high-ranking officer commented that the Macoutes would be transformed into army soldiers.

Worse still, on April 26, 1986, armed Tonton Macoutes reasserted their presence. They infiltrated and provoked violence at a memorial march of mostly elderly persons outside Fort Dimanche prison. Although the government arrested the Macoute leaders involved, this incident—which killed seven and injured thousands—focused discontent on Namphy.

"THE TRUE BIRTH OF ARISTIDE'S POLITICAL CAREER"

If the people were unhappy with Namphy, the general was equally unhappy with priest Jean-Bertrand Aristide. Raised in Port-au-Prince by a single mother, Aristide was a wisp of a man whose fragile body contrasted with the power of his voice and message. Aristide had spent much of his life working in the poorest bidonvilles, or shantytowns, fearlessly denouncing governmental abuse.

Namphy, however, felt Aristide was provoking people's dislike of him and planned a Macoute attack on Aristide's church congregation. According to one journalist,

> On September 11, [1988], at 9:15 A.M., Macoutes met at [Aristide's] St. Jean de Bosco Church . . . brandishing machetes, pointed sticks and guns. . . . They stormed inside chanting, "We will drink their blood." Father Aristide, protected by a group of his followers, escaped. Hundreds of his parishioners were not so lucky, and for the next two hours the Macoutes shot, beat, stabbed and slashed them, killing thirteen and wounding at least 77. . . . Outside, policemen stood by and watched as victims fled screaming from the church which the Macoutes then set on fire.[53]

Journalist Mark Danner describes this massacre as "the true birth of Aristide's political career—his metamorphosis

JEAN-BERTRAND ARISTIDE: POWERHOUSE IN A SMALL PACKAGE

Journalist Amy Wilentz, in an excerpt from her book *The Rainy Season: Haiti Since Duvalier*, recalls the first time she met Father Jean-Bertrand Aristide. It was 1986 and François "Baby Doc" Duvalier had just been sent into exile after prolonged popular protest.

I was soon joined by a man about whom I remembered little for a long time other than enormous glasses and a face like a bug, pop-eyed and watchful, a small, delicate man who looked even younger than the student I had sent off to find him. He had what appeared to be an eternal half-smile on his face. All the young men in the courtyard came and gathered around us, watching him intently.

"I'm Father Aristide," he said. "Can I help you?"

"Yes," I said. "That is, I think so. *You* seem happy."

"Well, I am, I am," he said smiling, showing crooked teeth. "We are all very happy here right now. We've been working on this for a long time, you know. All my life, in a way." He was thirty-two then.

"I don't know where to start," he said. "Where should I start?" He looked at the young men, who laughed. "Well, let's say this: We've been trying for a long time to figure out the best way to send away this government [Duvalier's]. Officially, my friends and I can't say that we've been organizing against the government, because we are in the Church. In other words, we are not doing politics, exactly, but what we are doing is trying to get a better life."

"He's been preaching against Duvalier," said the young man who had brought Aristide over to me. "A lot. For a long time. They didn't like it much. About a week ago, a guy came into the church, this Macoute from the neighborhood, and he had a revolver, he had it out. He shot it. He thought he could just come in here and shoot Father Aristide. But we did not permit that," he said. "We disarmed him, fast."

"We're glad Duvalier is gone," said Aristide. "That's why we seem so happy."

Jean-Bertrand Aristide

from priest to politician."[54] It also marked the end of Namphy's. Low-level soldiers, disgusted with the massacre—and the president's visible role in it—ousted Namphy. General Prosper Avril took over, claiming the soldiers had named him president.

Avril, though, had been a major administrator under the Duvaliers, and many Haitians were afraid he would rule the way Papa and Baby Doc had. As a result, Avril was in exile in Florida by March 1990, and Supreme Court judge Ertha Pascal-Trouillot took over as interim president. To her would fall the task of making sure presidential elections were held.

FREE, FAIR ELECTIONS

In 1990 the Organization of American States, headquartered in Washington, D.C., announced that it would send hundreds of international observers to Haiti to help the country hold free elections. Knowing the observers' presence would prohibit fixing election results, Aristide declared himself a candidate in October of that year. On December 16 Haitians poured into polling places. When the count was in, Aristide had taken a landslide 67 percent of the votes.

Taking office in February 1991, Aristide began to tackle Haiti's problems. He and his cabinet members attacked government corruption, negotiated new foreign aid, and, during what would become a brief "honeymoon" with the military, reduced the Tonton Macoutes' nightly killings.

The Haitian people loved Aristide, but he was not a politician. He did not know how to work with the National Assembly's elected legislators. And by not making it clear that he did not want the masses to resort to mob justice, Aristide nourished fear among the elite and army officers that the hungry, angry masses would riot in the streets. As a result, the elite and military ousted Aristide on September 30, 1991, and replaced him with General Raoul Cédras. (Aristide went first to Venezuela, then to the United States.)

The military and elite also transformed their fear into bloody vengeance, unleashing what would become three years of unrelenting repression against all of Haiti's poor, but particularly those who had helped organize efforts to elect Aristide. On the night of the coup, soldiers entered the bidonvilles with automatic weapons, mowing down anyone they saw. Refugees began pouring out of Haiti—nearly forty thousand in the first fifteen months of the military regime. Many others, fearing for their lives, went into hiding.

ARISTIDE RETURNS

From early in Aristide's exile, the U.S. government had tried to arrange for his return to office. U.S. officials did not know what to do with the thousands of Haitian refugees whom the U.S. Coast Guard had intercepted and taken to the American naval base in Guantánamo, Cuba. Likewise, human-rights and Haitian-American groups pressured the U.S. government and the United Nations (UN) to intervene to restore Aristide and prevent more bloodshed in Haiti.

In July 1994 the UN Security Council authorized the United States to use force to return Aristide to power. On September 19 U.S. and UN troops landed in Haiti. Aristide returned safely on October 15 to finish out his term's fourteen remaining months.

When Aristide's term ended in 1996, he was unable to run again due to a clause in Haiti's 1987 constitution prohibiting presidents from running for back-to-back terms. In that year's election only 15 percent of the electorate voted, and René Préval became Haiti's new president. Haitians apparently had lost hope in democracy. They had not been able to keep the leader they had elected in 1990 and instead had faced years of hardship and violence. That trend, unfortunately, continued.

"Five years after the U.S. invasion that restored Aristide to power, democracy has failed for most Haitians," reporter Catherine Orenstein wrote in 1999.

> The government has not functioned properly for over two years [due to quarreling by its various factions]. The most heinous crimes of the coup years remain unpunished. . . . Rising poverty and near-total impunity [powerful elements of the military and elite had not been brought to justice] have sharpened the longstanding fault lines that divide Haitian society.[55]

But this may not be the final word. Some changes begun under U.S. and UN leadership are taking root. Chief among these are reforms of the court system and the training of a new civilian police force. Furthermore, elections for thousands of legislators and local officials in May 2000 drew a re-

spectable turnout—an estimated 45 percent of Haiti's regis-
tered voters. Miraculously, election day was not marred by
violence.

Some saw the May 2000 elections as a sign of "a country
. . . tottering toward democracy,"[56] as journalist David Gonzalez put it. But no one can say for sure. Only time will tell
whether Haiti can pull itself out of its political instability and
emerge as an energetic modern nation.

*In 1994, U.S. troops
occupied Haiti to
guarantee Aristide's
return to power.*

4

DAILY LIFE IN HAITI

Lavi sé you pantalon défouké, san brétèl, sa—
sé lavi an Ayiti.
A pair of split pants with no suspenders; that—
is life in Haiti.

> —Edner A. Jeanty and O. Carl Brown,
> *Parol Granmoun: Haitian Popular Wisdom*

The United Nations now ranks Haiti among the world's poorest nations. "My country is not a country, it is a misery," a Haitian Roman Catholic priest remarked in 1986. "Before, people had no money, but they managed to eat. Now they don't eat."[57] Today the challenge to survive dictates most Haitians' daily lives.

THE RURAL FAMILY

Modern Haiti was born as a rural nation. After independence, former slaves preferred to stay on and work the land. As sociologist James G. Leyburn says, "The intimate observer of the Haitian peasant never fails to comment upon his love of the land. Whereas the colonial planter attached a value to his estate because it produced wealth, the peasant loves his little plot because it is his home."[58]

Peasants and their families form the backbone of rural Haiti, yet surprisingly, formal marriage is not the rule. This is probably because colonial planters thoroughly disapproved of marriage, a practice that might have presented obstacles to selling slaves. So today, as during the slave days, Haitian couples live together as if married, without going through legal formalities.

Haitian men are often polygynous, meaning they form unions with two or more women. One type of polygynous arrangement, in which the wives do not live together but have individual households "placed" throughout the countryside, is termed *plasaj*, or "placement." Leyburn believes *plasaj* developed in response to practical needs: "If a peasant increases his land holdings, if he buys or inherits a second farm on the other

side of the mountain, it is only common sense for him to take a second woman, raise a family by her, and thus have an overseer and a labor supply resident on each of his properties."[59]

THE *LAKOU*

Whatever their marriage arrangement, a rural couple's home usually forms part of a *lakou,* a horseshoe-shaped compound of extended family. The *lakou* is surrounded by walls of intertwining sticks and branches. Within the *lakou,* homes consist of wood-framed huts with thatch or corrugated-iron roofs. Furniture is minimal—a few chairs, a table, and some woven mats on which to sleep. According to one author, "The *lakou* in the Haitian countryside may seem poor and shabby but it is usually a warm and happy environment for children and a place for friendship and cooperation among adults. . . . It is the place where families gather to honor the spirits, celebrate births, mourn deaths, cook, eat, educate, and entertain, as in the telling of stories."[60]

Within the *lakou,* Haitians like to grow a few trees—usually fruit trees for quick snacks and/or ornamental trees for their shade and beauty. Families may also cultivate small

A Haitian family sits outside their home. In Haiti, marriages are often not formalized, and men may have more than one wife.

In addition to their responsibilities at home, Haitian women do most of the farming and operate all the open-air markets.

gardens in the *lakou* so that herbs and vegetables are close by. Their fields, rocky and hilly, are usually not very big and may total only one or one and a half hectares (three or four acres) or less. The fields are also often a one- to three-hour hike away.

RURAL WOMEN'S ROLES

Women are Haiti's workhorses, putting in long hours inside and outside the *lakou*. In addition to household chores, Haitian women perform much of the farm work and operate rural markets, carting goods from one area to another.

Despite women's hard work, they are often not given a say in important family and community decisions. In recent years, however, Haitian women have begun to recognize their potential and are organizing to counter old stereotypes and fight unfair treatment. According to a Haitian woman who helps organize rural women to work together to improve their well-being,

> Women run into several obstacles when they start to organize. First of all, they find obstacles at home. Some women have the support of their men, but some do not. We have a very male-dominated society here in Haiti,

and men believe that everything revolves around them. If women try to get out from under the system that dominates them, or if they try to get out of the controlling grasp of men, men begin to feel as if their lives are being threatened.[61]

HOME LIFE IN PORT-AU-PRINCE

Rural life in Haiti, though, for both men and women, is changing. Drought has made it harder to grow food and has forced many Haitians to move away from the farms. In general, men migrate to other countries—the United States, Canada, or other Caribbean islands—while women move to Haitian cities, particularly the capital.

What newcomers encounter in Port-au-Prince, however, is disheartening. More than half of the capital's residents live

---

A RETURN TO SLAVERY FOR SOME HAITIANS

Sometimes Haiti's impoverished children, especially those who are vulnerable because they are homeless and live on the street, are kidnapped and sold into slavery to cut sugarcane in the Dominican Republic. The testimony of eighteen-year-old Fatil, who was sold along with two friends, one of them only twelve, is reprinted here from *Teaching About Haiti*, edited by Catherine A. Sunshine and Deborah Menkart. The interview was conducted in Port-au-Prince in 1989, after Fatil had escaped and returned there.

One day a friend of ours came to see us, a guy named Jean Marc. He promised to take us to the capital of the Dominican Republic, Santo Domingo, where he thought we could find work. We accepted because we knew there was nothing positive here for us, and we trusted him. I called Eril and Ayiti [two friends], and we went along with him.

When we got to the border, we were told to get out of the car and continue on foot. We climbed a mountain and ended up at a military station in Jimani where we had to give our names and sit and wait. Jean Marc went for some water and never came back. We never saw him again.

Then we were told we weren't going to Santo Domingo, but to a *batey* [worker camp] to cut cane. We said we couldn't do that because we didn't know how. At that point we were told we had each been sold for 75 gourdes [about $15] to cut cane, and if we refused we would be thrown in jail. We had to agree.

We got to the *batey* and found out exactly what it was: heavy work. The leaves of the cane stalks cut us like blades. They told us if we returned to our country they would beat us, arrest us and throw us in jail.

in sprawling shantytowns without basic sanitation or services. Some of the largest bidonvilles include Cité Soleil, Bel-Air, Carrefour, Fort-National, and La Saline.

Homes in these slums are patchwork shacks of corrugated tin, cardboard, plastic sheeting, and other scavenged materials. Several families often share a single room. Journalist Amy Wilentz says housing is so crowded in the larger bidonvilles that people have to take turns sleeping, giving the illusion that Port-au-Prince's shantytowns never sleep. She describes the situation of the extended family—twelve adults and at least as many children—of a man named Djo:

Pictured is Cité Soleil, one of Port-au-Prince's largest shantytowns. Over half of the city's population live in neighborhoods like this one.

> Djo's house in Cité Soleil, the country's most populous slum, doesn't have the space for all these people, so usually when night falls they do a relève, or relay. First Djo and two brothers who have jobs that start early go to sleep; they sleep for four hours, maybe six, on the one bed in the one room of Djo's house. Meanwhile the other men sit up outside, playing dominoes and drinking herb teas at tables lit by candles or illuminated by

the spotlight of a single, bare bulb. . . . When Djo and
the two brothers get up, the other men go to sleep.[62]

EMPLOYMENT IN PORT-AU-PRINCE

Haitian women are often drawn to Port-au-Prince believing
they will find jobs. The World Bank, however, lists Haiti's 1999
unemployment rate at a whopping 70 percent, although a lim-
ited number of factory jobs are available in Port-au-Prince. Beginning in the late 1960s, Jean-Claude "Baby Doc" Duvalier
opened Haiti to foreign-owned assembly plants, also known
as *maquilas,* or "sweatshops." These industries employ mostly
young women in their teens and twenties to assemble items
from materials that are brought into the country.

The pay in these factories is not good, and the items the
workers produce are not sold in Haitian markets. In 1999
most *maquilas* paid workers the minimum wage of $2.40 for
an eight-hour day, or 30¢ an hour. The finished goods, usually
clothing, are shipped elsewhere for sale. In 1996, for example, Haitian women were sewing clothing for sale in Wal-
Mart, J. C. Penney, Kmart, Kids R Us, and other retailers.

The factories also come and go easily, creating job insecurity. In 1990, for instance, some fifty thousand Haitians
were employed in *maquilas,* but many companies left during
the political chaos following the military coup that ousted
President Aristide. In the years since, the number of Haitians
working in *maquilas* has dropped to roughly twenty-five
thousand, but economists expect the number to increase
again as the political situation stabilizes.

Women *maquila* workers often find that their pay covers
just their own expenses—transportation and a small lunch—
leaving nothing for their families. In 1998 some women
workers explained their dilemma:

> When you are working at the factory, the small amount
> of money that you get paid is only enough to eat at the
> factory. You don't make enough money to take home, let
> alone think about starting some savings. The 36 *goud*
> [gourdes] (U.S. $2.40) you receive for the day's work, you
> have already spent at the factory to feed yourself. You
> can't do anything else with it. And you have to dress, you
> have children to send to school, you have rent to pay.
> They give you 36 *goud* for an eight-hour day.[63]

Because of poverty, rural families often send their children to the city to work as restavecs, *unpaid servants in the homes of wealthy families.*

In addition to factory work, some women work as domestics—cooks, nannies, and maids—for wealthier families. Because of Haiti's racial divisions, these often dark-skinned household helpers are usually treated poorly by lighter-skinned employers. Many observers have noted that the Haitian elite often view household helpers with contempt. Household helpers usually earn less than *maquila* workers—fifteen to twenty gourdes per day.

CHILD DOMESTIC WORKERS: *RESTAVECS*

During the 1990s increased hunger in Haiti's countryside—a result of political upheaval—caused parents to send their children to city families to work as household servants. This custom of giving children to wealthier families so they may eat and perhaps have a better life dates back to the country's birth in 1804. For parents, it is a last resort, providing a glimmer of hope that their children will survive. Yet these rural parents do not comprehend the disastrous emotional fate that awaits their children in the cities.

Unpaid child servants are known as *restavecs*; the term comes from the French *rester avec,* meaning "to stay with someone." It is not as inviting as it sounds, however. The children, some as young as four, become virtual slaves in

RESTAVEC

The following is excerpted from *Restavec: From Haitian Slave Child to Middle-Class American.* Author Jean-Robert Cadet—who was a *restavec,* or unpaid child servant—recalls his fervent wish that Florence, the woman whom he worked for, would buy him clothes and plan a meal for his upcoming First Communion.

[Florence] walked in without saying a word. I went inside and fetched her slippers. She changed into another dress and began to supervise the cook. In the early afternoon, after I finished my chores, I approached Florence with a pail of water and a towel and began to wash her feet. She was sitting in her rocking chair, sipping sweet hot black coffee from a saucer. With pounding heart, I spoke. "Confession is at six o'clock and Communion is tomorrow at nine o'clock in the morning."

She stared at me for a long moment as she ground her teeth. Her face turned very angry, ". . . If you think I'm gonna spend my money on your First Communion, you're insane," she shouted. Trembling with fear, I dried her feet and stood up. I felt as though my feet and legs were too heavy for me to move. I was stunned by her words. "Get out of my face," she yelled. I went into the kitchen and sat quietly in my usual corner without shedding a tear.

"Amelia!" called Florence loudly.

"Oui [yes], Madame Cadet," the cook responded.

"You don't need to prepare the chicken for tomorrow; I'm spending the day with my niece. Her son is having his First Communion tomorrow," she said. . . .

I felt crushed, but at the same time resigned myself to believe that only children with real mothers and fathers go to First Communion, receive presents from Santa Claus, and celebrate their birthdays.

exchange for food and shelter. Worse perhaps than their duties are the attitudes they face; *restavecs* are Haiti's "untouchables." The United Nations Children's Fund estimates that three hundred thousand *restavecs* work in Haiti, one-fifth of them between the ages of seven and ten, although many more likely remain unreported.

One Haitian man describes the *restavec* lifestyle:

> A child domestic has many responsibilities. They get up the earliest, sometimes as early as 4 A.M. to fetch water, to wash dishes.

> Let's talk about where they sleep. On rags, on cardboard, on the floor. They don't have a right to a room. They sleep in a hallway, in a kitchen. They sweep, make coffee, go to the market for breakfast food for the family, start the day's cooking.

> These children have no time to themselves. Sometimes they go into a corner to try to take a nap. If they're caught they will be kicked and told they are lazy. The idea is to keep them with the mentality that they have no worth. If they're really sick, they are sent home [to their families].

> They don't eat out of the same pot as the others. They eat what the families consider to be the second-class food, leftover cornmeal with a little bean sauce.

> They don't exist as people. They don't have a right to play with the household children.[64]

Because Haitian law requires that children over age fifteen be paid to work, many wealthy families turn the *restavecs* out when they turn fifteen rather than pay them. In most cases, the children then join other working children in the streets.

STREET CHILDREN

Many Haitian children work in the streets and marketplaces, hoping to earn enough to eat. While Haitian law prohibits children under fifteen from working, hundreds of thousands have no choice. City children perform odd jobs, including carting heavy items for market women, washing windshields, shining shoes, helping to load Haiti's tap-taps (buses), and selling items.

Wealthy Haitians do not like these children because they beg and often steal. Children's advocates such as Godfry "Gody" Boursiquot, though, try to explain that street children

WALDEK, A HAITIAN TEEN

Emily Wade Will met a young boy named Waldek Derisma during a visit to Haiti in 1993; the following is based on their chats.

Chak koukouy klere pour je li.
Each lightning bug lights the way only for itself.
(Haitian Proverb)

Haitians do not admire lightning bugs, symbols of self-centeredness in a society where people must depend on others. Waldek Derisma, 13, is no lightning bug. He spends most of his day helping his parents and four siblings get by in their town in Haiti's northeast.

Upon awakening Waldek locates his family's three goats and ties them near greenery, where they will eat all day. If one has broken its rope and strayed, he will search for it—for minutes, hours, or all day. Waldek then scavenges for firewood. He may scour the hillsides for up to two hours to find the basketful needed to cook the day's meals; this often makes him late for school.

When school lets out at 1 o'clock, Waldek eats his first meal of the day, usually rice and beans. He cares for baby sister, Veniz, in the afternoon. He feeds her porridge and takes her to the market so their mother can nurse her.

Waldek's mother sells fritters, called *marinad*, at the market. Most days she earns enough to buy two to four plates of beans and rice. On Tuesdays, when people from nearby villages overflow the market, she earns more.

Late afternoons Waldek runs errands. He fills the family's water jugs at the community pipe and delivers clothes to people who hire his mother to wash them. Before supper, Waldek moves the goats to fresh brush; they eat throughout the night, between naps. The goats serve as a savings account. When unexpected expenses arise, the Derismas sell one.

Waldek wants to farm his own land when he is grown. But for now, he is content—and nobody accuses **him** of being a lightning bug!

Waldek Derisma holds his baby sister, Veniz.

are merely surviving, and that they are adept, if not ingenious, at making do in undesirable, even hostile, circumstances:

> Kids are like grass. They take root. Wherever they find themselves, they adapt. On the street, they live with their friends. They may sleep in cars, under porches, under bridges. They work at small jobs to live. If they are described as vicious little brats, or dirty, it is not because this is their natural way. They are doing what they need to do to survive.[65]

Street children look out for one another. At various times, for example, police officers or Tonton Macoutes have waged cleanup campaigns against street children. "[Before], soldiers would pick them up, beat them, hurt them, sometimes kill them," says Boursiquot, who hosts a children's radio show in which children talk about their lives. "One child would be the guard, to watch for police and sirens all night, to wake the others. The threat is still there, but not so much."[66]

RELIGION

Haiti's religious communities, both Roman Catholic and Protestant, have traditionally worked on behalf of children, running orphanages and schools. In the absence of governmental services, these religious groups have supplied many community needs. Haiti's indigenous religion, Vodun, though, does not provide social services as much as it gives Haitians an anchor for understanding their world.

The Haitian constitution allows for religious freedom, and almost all Haitians practice Vodun (also known as Voodoo); a great majority—70 to 80 percent—are also Roman Catholic. Most Haitians who practice Vodun are comfortable mixing this religion with Roman Catholicism. The Catholic Church disagrees, however, and does not think worship of Vodun gods is consistent with Catholic doctrine.

The word *Vodun* means "Spirit" and comes from the language of the Fon, a people indigenous to the African nation now called Benin. Hundreds of spirits or gods, called *lwa*, exist in Vodun, each with its own personality. Some *lwa* have human representations; others do not. Among the most widely known are Damballa, giver of rain, symbolized by the serpent; Ogun, god of war; Erzuli, wealthy goddess of love and beauty, who resembles the Virgin Mary in Haitian representations; Legba, guardian of crossroads and highways; and Baron Samedi, spirit watchman of cemeteries.

Many Catholics and Protestants view this Vodun pantheon of *lwa* as a direct contradiction to the belief in a single, all-mighty God. In Vodun belief, however, one spirit created the world and rules supreme over the other spirits. For this reason, African slaves raised with Vodun had little, if any, problem accepting the Christian God. They named this greater spirit Bondye, or "Good God." Other features of Vodun include spirit possession (the belief that a spirit enters a person's body and causes him or her to act differently), drumming and religious dancing, and animal sacrifice.

Vodun religious services have two parts. The first part is a churchlike service within the *hounfor*, or temple. The second is an outdoor dance, with throbbing drums. Presiding over Vodun services are *houngans*, or priests, and *mambos*, or priestesses.

The religion has adapted over the years, borrowing ideas and rites from Catholicism and other influences. This flexibility may help explain why it has endured so solidly among Haiti's masses. As Leyburn puts it, "Vodun lacks a formal theology. No seminary exists for the training of priests and priestesses. . . . No scriptures or sermons are printed or read. . . . Vodun is an informal religion of action, not a formal

A group of Haitian women participate in an outdoor Vodun ceremony.

one of reason. It flourishes because it is malleable, adaptive, suited to the needs of a people living close to nature and without education."[67]

Perhaps the nighttime drumming, heard in Haiti's faraway hills, and the animal sacrifice have caused outsiders to think of Vodun as a religion of superstitions. To the contrary, anthropologist Wade Davis claims that

> Vodun is not an isolated cult; it is a complex mystical worldview, a system of beliefs concerning the relationship between humankind, nature, and the supernatural forces of the universe. It fuses the unknown to the known, creates order out of chaos, renders the mysterious intelligible. Vodun cannot be abstracted from the day-to-day lives of the believers. In Haiti, as in Africa, there is no separation between the sacred and the secular, between the holy and the profane, between the material and the spiritual.[68]

As a worldview, Vodun offers consolation and rationale to a people whose circumstances are grim. Vodun explains why bad things happen even to innocent and good people. Haitians believe that when misfortune befalls the Vodun follower, it is because he or she has displeased a *lwa*. The question then becomes how to appease the spirit.

VODUN SPIRIT-HUMAN INTERACTION

Vodun believers often interact closely with the *lwa*, almost as if they were family, as scholar Donald Cosentino explains:

> Because the *lwa* are close to humans, they enjoy human hospitality. Therefore, during a *Vodun* ceremony, the people may sacrifice a small farm animal, often a chicken or goat, to them. Afterward, the worshipers cook and eat the animal. To attract more divine attention, servants of the *lwa* draw special emblems, called *veve*, on the floors of the *hounfors* [temples] and dance and sing their favorite songs.

> The *lwa* communicate with their servants through a spiritual possession of their minds and bodies. . . . It is said that the *lwa* ride their servants like horses and sometimes are called divine horsemen. When a worshiper is being ridden, he or she speaks and acts like the

A FARM WOMAN TELLS HER STORY

Antwanèt, who lives in Haiti's Artibonite Valley, relates the challenges facing farm women like herself in the book *Like the Dew That Waters the Grass: Words from Haitian Women,* by Marie M. B. Racine and Kathy Ogle.

Women participate fully in all of the farming activities. We clear the ground, pull the weeds, plant the seeds and replant the seedlings when they are bigger. We women also spread the fertilizer. Then the rice grows. The men beat the rice, and the women thresh the rice [separate the seed from the plant]. The women put the rice in bags and take the bags to the closest mill. We dry the rice for three days, then we thresh it and grind it. We measure it, and we bag it again. Then we pay a man to carry the bags to a truck so that we can take it to the market to be sold there—like in Pòto-prens [Port-au-Prince]. When we arrive at the market, we put the rice in a storage place. Sometimes, we can't find a storage place and we have to keep it on the streets with us, and so we sleep on the bags.

Here are some of the miseries we get from sleeping on top of the bag: We are bitten by mosquitoes. We are soaked by the rain. Our feet are sunk into the mud, and insects that are in the mud get on our feet. They even come inside our underwear. There are times when we get a fever in the market. Despite all of those things, we may not even come back with any money. Sometimes we return with only the [empty] bags. Why? The money has been stolen! After going through all of these problems, sometimes we lose everything!

Perhaps we had sent our children to school and had not yet paid for that, and perhaps the debt that we incurred in order to generate more money has not yet been paid. Our husband has been waiting for us to come back with the money. The children are waiting for some candy from their mother's trip. Everyone starts crying. Mother, children, father. It's the woman's misery. The money is lost. That's the situation of rural women who work the land in the Atibonit [Artibonite].

lwa. . . . Afterward, the person who was possessed cannot remember the experience.[69]

TI LEGLIZ

In the 1960s the Roman Catholic Church was recognizing that many people in many countries lacked education, health services, food, clothing, and housing. In 1962 top church officials began adapting Catholic doctrine to address these problems. For example, the church said the oppression and poverty affecting many people around the world was not what God had in mind for the human race. What God wants for people, the church claimed, is liberation—the freedom to live with dignity. This new thought became known as "liberation theology," and it spread to Haiti in the 1970s, where it was called *Ti Legliz*, or "Little Church."

Ti Legliz became a strong force for change in Haiti. Priests and nuns spoke out against the abuses of the government and the elites. It led many Haitians to believe they did not need to be passive victims of a cruel social system. Today *Ti Legliz* reaches out to all Haitians, regardless of their faith. According to one active church member,

> The *Ti Legliz* began, of course, within the Roman Catholic Church, but . . . they opened up the ranks . . . because they realized that whatever the person's religious tradition was—whether Catholic, Protestant or the practice of *vodou* [Vodun]—they faced the same problems. This was especially apparent in the poor neighborhoods. Whatever their beliefs, people had a desire to assemble in a community and share their sufferings.[70]

AN UNEDUCATED POPULATION

The *Ti Legliz* movement also hoped that the Haitian government would step in and assume responsibility for helping to meet the people's needs. To date, that has not happened, and church groups—from within Haiti and from other countries—continue to fill the void until the government is able to do so.

One void is in education. Although Haiti has some public schools, they are few, and the teaching is poor. Consequently, citizens of one of the poorest nations must pay to send their children to private, often church-run schools. Even if fees are kept low and few supplies are required, the costs are prohibitive for many families.

Whether a child attends school probably matters little in the long run, however. Most schools are hopelessly understaffed and are ill equipped to prepare today's children for their future. Journalist Amy Wilentz describes a typical Haitian school: "The school is run by a twenty-one-year-old teacher who teaches his Kreyòl-speaking students in French, even though they can't speak it and his own French is negligible. The schoolbooks date from early in Papa Doc's rule. Most teachers in the Haitian countryside, and many in town, are subliterate."[71]

SOCIAL PROGRAMS

Recognizing that the lack of education plays a prominent role in Haiti's deteriorating economic and social situation,

many international agencies have tried to teach Haitians to fend for themselves through community programs in adult education and literacy, by training midwives and health workers, through reforestation and agriculture, and through various community self-help projects. Additionally, to reduce dependency on foreigners, many agencies first train Haitian personnel who, in turn, work with their neighbors.

However, such programs are long-term, requiring years to get up and running, and Haiti is a country that needs help right away. As a result many of these programs are still in the planning stages. Due to the political upheaval of the 1990s, along with Haiti's severe ecological decay, many agencies had to divert their priorities from long-term to immediate programs to help a nation on the verge of starvation.

International relief agencies feed about 1 million Haitians daily, and they have had to concentrate on helping the locals survive one day at a time. For many Haitians, it is a struggle, one with no easy solution but which they are determined to overcome.

Schoolchildren in Port-au-Prince wait for classes to start. Unfortunately, the majority of schools in Haiti are unable to provide children with an adequate education.

5

HAITIAN ARTS AND MUSIC

Dan ri malè.
Haitians laugh even when they should cry.
—Edner A. Jeanty and O. Carl Brown,
Parol Granmoun: Haitian Popular Wisdom

No matter how miserable Haiti's political and economic conditions, Haitian culture not only survives but also thrives. Poverty has not been able to extinguish the vitality of Haitian imagination and creativity, which flowers in Haiti's arts and music. As the authors of one book write, "Haiti is a political failure but a cultural success."[72]

THE PROVERBIAL HAITIAN

Among the large body of Haitian folklore, proverbs and storytelling stand out. Even illiterate Haitians pepper their conversation with colorful proverbs, reflecting their hard-earned wisdom. Proverbs are "one of the things Haitians like most,"[73] says Edner A. Jeanty, who jotted down adages he heard throughout his country. He notes that Haiti's proverbs speak to pressing daily concerns—earning a living, facing inequality, and finding contentment in events large and small.

As many as fifteen hundred Haitian proverbs have been collected, and many more likely exist. *Dèyè mòn gen mòn*—behind the mountains, more mountains—is a frequently quoted Haitian proverb. It describes the country's geography while also illustrating Haitians' dilemma: As soon as they have conquered one mountainous problem, they face another.

KRIK? KRAK!

In Haiti, night is the appropriate time for storytelling; superstition holds that misfortune awaits those who spend daylight hours telling tales. Beyond that, adds scholar Jean Price-Mars, the Haitian tale "begs for the mystery of the night to mute the rhythmic narrative and to place the action in the realm of enchantment."[74]

Haitian storytelling begins with a ritual. Storytellers signal their readiness to begin by asking *"Krik?"*—meaning, "Shall I tell you a story?" or, "Are you ready?" The audience responds with *"Krak!"*—"Yes, we are listening."

Effective storytellers employ acting skills. They perform the story, giving each character a voice, and often singing songs as part of the tale. One anthropologist who has collected Haitian folktales writes, "Storytellers in the rural sections are experts at mimicry and pantomime, and their representations of animals, neighbors, foreigners, and prominent Haitians are almost perfect."[75] Sometimes the storyteller acts more as a director, involving the listeners, especially children, in singing, producing sound effects, and narrating some of the tale.

UNCLE BOUKI AND TI MALIS

Among the most popular Haitian tales are the adventures of two inseparable characters, Uncle Bouki and Ti Malis. Uncle Bouki is a cordial country bumpkin, often foolish but also stubbornly trying to avoid being duped. Ti Malis, a mischievous trickster, generally gets the better of Uncle Bouki.

Price-Mars suggests that Uncle Bouki may have been modeled on the slave newly arrived in Saint Domingue, fresh from Africa, ignorant of his new surroundings. Ti Malis, on the other hand, represents someone born in Saint Domingue and who knows his way around. His superior knowledge of the ways things work puts Ti Malis in a position to take advantage of Uncle Bouki's naïveté—and he does so at every opportunity.

Historians propose that the name *Bouki* is derived from an African tribe known as the Bouriqui. The Bouriqui were not submissive and proved generally unwilling to accommodate to colonial life—unlike some other African peoples who more easily assimilated into the slave masses. With time, Uncle Bouki came to symbolize "a certain strength forged of patience, resignation and intelligence, the expression of which is revealed in the masses of our mountain peasants,"[76] writes Price-Mars.

PAINTING

Haitians also reveal their patience, resignation, and intelligence—as well as their overflowing reservoir of imagination

TI MALIS, UNCLE BOUKI, AND SWEET POTATOES

Uncle Bouki, the country bumpkin, and Ti Malis, the mischievous trickster, are Haitians' enduring and endearing folktale characters. Their exploits have been recounted on starry nights throughout the countryside since Haiti's birth as a modern nation and probably even during its tormented days of slavery. This tale is taken from *Haiti: Teacher's Guide*, published by the Mennonite Central Committee in 1996.

Ti Malis woke up one morning and said, "I have not seen my Uncle Bouki for a while. I'm going to stop by his house this morning. Perhaps he is sick."

Malis went to Bouki's house. When he got there, Bouki was cooking some sweet potatoes. Malis greeted Bouki and took a seat. He would not leave without eating some sweet potatoes with his Uncle Bouki. But after waiting four hours, Ti Malis finally asked Bouki, "What are you cooking? It has been on the fire since I arrived and you haven't taken it off."

Uncle Bouki said to him, "Ah, it is nothing. It is only some sweet potatoes I gathered in the garden this morning. But they are not good. They have sweet potato disease. Let me look at them again." Bouki bent down and pretended to look into the cooking pot. He rose and said, "Too bad for you, Ti Malis. I would give you some but they are not good."

Malis said, "Is it true, Uncle Bouki? Okay, if they have sweet potato disease, you cannot eat them. Let me throw them out for you."

Malis took the cooking pot of sweet potatoes and threw them out. He said, "Let me pound them with my feet so the dog won't eat them. It is the sweet potato disease that killed the neighbors' dog." Malis pounded them with his feet and said to Bouki, "I'm going now, Uncle Bouki. I will see you another day."

After Malis left, Bouki scratched his head and said, "If I had given Malis some of my sweet potatoes, this would not have happened to me and I wouldn't have lost them all."

and hopes—in paint. When they do not have canvases, they produce murals on the sides of *hounfors*, shops, and taptaps. Much of their painting carries religious significance. As historians Robert Debs Heinl Jr. and Nancy Gordon Heinl put it, "Just as the artisans of Europe's Gothic cathedrals worked solely for the greater glory of God, these peasant artists were painting to please their *lwa*, and the *lwa* must indeed have been pleased."[77]

In the mid-1940s paintings by Haitians trying to please their *lwa* found their way into the world limelight. The story behind this unexpected happening starts with a Californian named Dewitt Peters. During World War II Peters applied for conscientious-objector status, granted via application to the U.S. government, so he could serve without a weapon. (Conscientious objectors refuse to bear arms based on moral or religious grounds). In 1943 the U.S. Alternative Service program sent him to Haiti to teach English.

Having studied art in both New York and Paris, Peters soon began dreaming of a Haitian center for the arts, a place where local artists could receive instruction and exhibit their work. Within a month of his arrival, Peters approached the Haitian Ministry of Education, and in May 1944, the Centre d'Art was inaugurated in Port-au-Prince. Today it functions as a museum.

Peters later recorded the enthusiasm and success of the center's early years:

> What my young Haitian collaborators—artists and intellectuals—and I could not know in those exciting days . . . when we [first began our work] was the amount of talent which lay buried, not aware even of its own existence, in the so-called lower classes. Two and a half years later, a group of Haitian paintings was sent off, without fanfare or great expectations, to the international exhibition of painting that was organized by UNESCO [the United Nations Educational, Scientific, and Cultural Organization] in Paris. I will never forget that morning when I casually opened the latest copy of Time [magazine] and, turning first to the page on art, read with rising excitement and emotion the report from Paris: Little Haiti's contribution had taken the international art world by storm—my "primitive" friends had stolen the show![78]

UNSCHOOLED OR "PRIMITIVE" ARTISTS

During his first years in Haiti, Peters located individuals with promising talent and offered them support to develop their skills. Doing so was tricky; he did not want to change their style, which was fresh, spontaneous, and untouched by world influences. It was more a matter of refining or polishing their techniques and providing materials and ample encouragement.

Peters's approach, nonjudgmental and low-key, was likely the only approach that would have allowed him, a white foreigner, to win Haitians' trust. And there were many reasons for the Haitians not to trust him. Many would still have had memories of American racism during the occupation. When the Haitian Ministry of Education donated a building to his cause, Peters was probably unaware that its location in a wealthy neighborhood might cause some poor Haitians to feel uncomfortable visiting it. Yet despite these obstacles, Peters and his artists thrived. The Haitians' work, within only years of Peters's arrival, was displayed in some of the world's leading art museums and brought art dealers from around the globe to Port-au-Prince. Peters describes some of his first contacts with those artists:

> The unearthing of the popular or natural painters [untaught artists] was slow work, requiring tact and affection. Mostly from the masses, they were timid about coming into the impressive, cream-colored building, once a private home, in the center of the city and set back from the street by a charming garden. The first to venture was Philomé Obin. Late in 1944 he sent us, by a relative, a small, naïve painting, *The Arrival of President Roosevelt to Lift the American Occupation of Haiti.* It was my first experience of a Haitian popular painting,

A Haitian artist paints in his studio. Despite their humble circumstances, Haitian artists produce amazing works of art.

and I was not too sure how to take it. I compromised by sending the artist a letter with a five-dollar bill and a package of art materials to a value of another five. Today Obin is considered by most foreign critics to be one of the great natural realists of contemporary painting.[79]

Peters also traveled into the countryside, where he met a Vodun priest, Hector Hyppolite, who earned his living as a house painter in Saint Marc. Hyppolite used leftover house enamel to paint Vodun gods and flamboyant flowers and fruits on the walls of his *hounfor*. Peters convinced Hyppolite to move to Port-au-Prince, and as art historian Ute Stebich relates, "for almost three years, [Hyppolite] painted in a splendid kind of exaltation literally hundreds of pictures. This incredibly creative production was, of course, uneven. But at his rich, inspired best, Hyppolite remains one of the greatest natural painters of modern times."[80]

THEMES

Peters—who remained in Haiti until his death in 1966—encouraged untrained artists to continue to express their community values and traditional beliefs. Not surprisingly, then, the themes they painted with such vitality revolved around Haiti's history since the slave uprising, or depicting nature, daily life, and Vodun.

These themes remain central to Haitian art, and the emotion artists most often try to convey is joy—exuberant, irrepressible joy. Given Haiti's political and economic misery, the joy of Haitian art is both a mystery and a great gift to the world. Selden Rodman, who became codirector of the Centre d'Art in 1947 and who remained active in Haiti's arts through at least the 1980s, believes the joy Haitians express in their art arises from inner peace and an ability to glory in the here and now without guilt, regret, or fear. Writing in 1988, Rodman asked,

Why are the Haitian people almost alone in the world today in feeling this *rapport* [harmony] with things as they are and in reflecting so much joy through their art? . . . Nowhere has a whole "school" of art, the dominant, self-taught art of a nation, embodied such values—and done so consistently over a period of more than forty years—as in Haiti.[81]

This painting by Hector Hyppolite titled Agoué and his Wife, *depicts the Vodun god of the sea and his spouse, La Sirène, the sea* lwa *of love.*

Rodman believes the answer to his own question resides in Haitians' pride in their history and the importance of their religion. "If *vaudou* [Vodun] does vanish, the special arts of Haiti may vanish with it,"[82] he predicts.

BEYOND THE CENTRE D'ART

Although Vodun has not vanished from Haitian art, its influence has diminished over the years as paintings have become commercialized and geared toward themes that interest tourists. According to Rodman, "When the dry rot of commercialism began to intrude, the center of gravity shifted effortlessly."[83]

The last generation of untrained artists, all Vodun-inspired, was intentionally developed in the 1970s in the town of Soissons la Montagne, outside of Port-au-Prince. These five primitive artists became known as the Saint-Soleil painters. The group was brought together by two intellectuals of the elite class, Tiga Garoute and Maud Robart. They hoped to achieve results similar to those attained by Peters and others, who offered materials and encouragement, but not outright advice, to peasant artists.

Among the five Saint-Soleil painters was Louisiane St. Fleurant, generally considered the first poor Haitian woman to receive material and moral support similar to that offered to men. With the exception of St. Fleurant, Luce Turnier of the elite class, and a few other women, Haitian painting and sculpture have been almost exclusively dominated by men.

Louisiane St. Fleurant's often large canvases employ a technique reminiscent of the sixth-century Byzantines, who embedded fragments of gold enameling in their productions to catch the light and thus honor their saints and gods. St. Fleurant expanded on this technique, combining flecks of color that add a unique, vibrant illumination to the religious imagery that takes center stage in her paintings.

NONPRIMITIVE ARTISTS

St. Fleurant, untrained, paints in the primitive style. Today, however, some Haitian painters are trying to move beyond the primitive style, but they say it is difficult. The public has trouble accepting styles not based on traditions established by the "primitives." Among these painters is fifty-year-old Enock Placide, who now lives in Long Island, New York.

Placide began to paint at age twelve, after watching an artist paint the organ doors of Holy Trinity Cathedral in Port-au-Prince. To encourage Placide, a nun who noticed his interest provided him with a steady supply of paint, paper, and brushes. In the late 1960s he became involved in a movement known as the Gallery Brochette, an organization that encouraged nonprimitive painters. He was drawn to the Gallery Brochette because, says Placide, "Centre d'Art produced a stereotyping of Haitian art. When you limit the scope of an artist, you are denying the right of expression."[84]

Additionally, some artists, although they are few and far between, have chosen to paint political-themed works. These are rare simply because the volatile political situation makes it dangerous. Favrange Valcin, whose paintings since the

1960s have depicted subjects including neglected servants, unwanted children, refugees, and the murderous Tonton Macoutes, is the most famous in this genre.

Regardless of the theme, though, many people today do not believe Haitian art swings only to the side of the primitives. In fact, they contend, the range of styles produced in Haiti is wide, and most people now accept any art done by Haitians as "Haitian" despite whether it is primitive.

SCULPTURE

Along with Haiti's painting renaissance of the mid-1900s, interest blossomed in sculpture. Sculptors such as Odilon Duperrier used native woods, namely mahogany and oak, to create expressive three-dimensional tableaus of people and their surroundings. Likewise, André Dimanche, a peasant, carved haunting figures from twisted tree roots. More recently, metal sculpture began to flourish in Haiti. A blacksmith from the town of Croix-des-Bouquets, Georges Liataud, revolutionized the metal arts in the 1950s when he flattened oil drums and produced extraordinary two-dimensional figures by cutting, hammering, and texturing the steel sheets. Today many workshops, even small factories, throughout

EXCHANGING CLEANING RAGS AND BROOMS FOR CANVASES AND BRUSHES

Louisiane St. Fleurant was working as a domestic servant when her artistic ability was discovered. In a 1996 interview with Marie M. B. Racine and Kathy Ogle, authors of *Like the Dew That Waters the Grass: Words from Haitian Women*, St. Fleurant relates her story.

I used to do housework and cook for a living. In fact, when I started working with Madan [Madame] Woba, I used to cook for her. I used to prepare food. I used to clean houses. I used to wash clothes. That was a lot of hard work! But that was the work I was used to doing.

But then one day in 1972, Madan Woba bought paper and asked me to draw. She liked what I did, so I continued to do more drawings and paintings. I worked with Madan and Msye [Monsieur] Woba and with Tiga, a man who started an art school at Swason [a town near Port-au-Prince] and I began to learn about painting.

I didn't know anything about paintings or exhibits. It was Tiga and Madan Woba who taught me about these things. It is thanks to them that I can make a living. When I realized I didn't need to go to people's houses to work and that I could sell my paintings, I decided to give all my time to painting.

Haiti produce cut-metal sculptures. Some are vast wall-size murals; others are small, colorful pieces made specifically for tourists.

Because they have access to so few natural resources, Haitian sculptors must use discarded, low-cost materials—and they do so with flair. Large, intricate cemetery wreaths, for example, are created out of discarded tin cans. Another versatile material, papier-mâché, is made from cement bags and glue extracted from the starch of the manioc, a root grown widely on the island since the time of the indigenous Taíno. Artists use papier-mâché most often for small sculptures and whimsical carnival masks, usually painted in bright colors.

Three men perform a traditional dance on a street in Port-au-Prince. Since colonial times, dance has been an integral part of Haitian society.

VODUN MUSIC AND DANCE

Like the early arts, music and dance in Haiti have traditionally been an integral part of religious celebration. According to Harold Courlander, who traveled throughout Haiti collecting folk music,

> In the hills of Haiti everyone sings and dances. Babies of three years dance Vodun and Pétro [religious dances] with their elders. Boys of seven are already master

drummers under the teaching of their fathers, who learned from their own fathers. And old women weighed down by years and infirmities still dance Ibo [also a religious dance] with their shoulders.[85]

Most colonial planters did not understand the relationship between dance and religion. They thought the word *Vodun* referred only to a vigorous dance. Vodun worshipers indeed dance with zeal but it is with the purpose of seeking the spirits' inspiration, guidance, and protection. Had the colonists known that the drumming they heard was not just providing rhythm for the Vodun dances but was also being used to communicate with other slaves on distant plantations, they may not have permitted the dances. In fact, Haiti's slave revolt was hatched during Vodun ceremonies.

A Vodun service consists of two parts—the first is ceremonial and ritualistic officiated over by priests inside the *hounfor*, or temple. The second part is a celebratory dance, held outdoors. According to sociologist James G. Leyburn,

> The dance has all the appearance of a social event. Invitations to it are sent all over the countryside. People attend for good fellowship, gossip, and the sheer delight of dancing, but in the background one is always aware of a religious element as well. The dance is held in a specially constructed *tonnelle*, a roof of boughs and leaves supported by uprights. Drums are not always used at the earlier service, but no dance could be held without them. The crowd drifts in slowly, so that the dance may be long in getting under way. The best drummers in the community may not arrive until after two or three hours. Three drums of different sizes set the rhythms, and sometimes gourd rattles embroider a commentary upon [accompany] the beat.[86]

The drums are considered sacred. The largest drum is called *manman*, the medium-size one is referred to as *seconde*, and the smallest is the *bula* or *kata*. In addition to the continuous drumming, the dance is accompanied by call-and-response singing, in which the singer calls out a word or phrase and the audience responds by singing it back.

Since slave times, observers have noted that even the most laborious work all day long under a hot sun does not interfere with Haitians' enthusiasm for dance, nor does it apparently limit their energy for it. The dances, instead, lift the Haitians' spirits and help them endure their difficult lives.

CARNIVAL MUSIC AND DANCE

Dance and music of a nonreligious nature take over during Mardi Gras, or Carnival, when bands of masked dancers, called *rara*, converge on the country's streets. Many of the *rara* dances are sexually suggestive or lewd, and many require great agility. Dancers are accompanied by musicians playing bamboo trumpets called *vaccines*. Wade Davis provides a memorable description of the *rara* bands:

> The town was . . . in a frenzy. It was Easter, and the Rara bands had swarmed out of the temples to celebrate the end of Lent [a religious holiday]. Their processions wove through the streets, swirling past one another, invading gardens and homes, absorbing idlers and growing longer and longer tails of dancers. From a distance they could be taken as hallucinations, except for the

Masked dancers, or rara, *dance during Carnival in Port-au-Prince.*

music—a single four-note song. Tin cans transformed into trumpets and trombones created a glittering horn section; rubber hose transformed into tubas created another. Percussion in the hands of a Haitian is anything that knocks—two sticks, a hubcap, a hammer-and-leaf spring from a truck.[87]

KOMPA: SOCIAL DANCE MUSIC

In Haitian cities and towns, as well as in the rural areas, people also gather for purely social dances called *bambouches.* A popular Caribbean music heard at these social dances is *kompa.*

Kompa was created in 1955 by noted Haitian composer, guitarist, saxophonist, and bandleader Jean-Baptiste Nemours. Nemours adapted merengue (a fast type of dance and music popular in many countries) by slowing the tempo and simplifying the melodies. In just two years *kompa* had become Haiti's prominent dance music, and it remained so through the 1980s. People particularly liked it because it was easy to dance to.

VODUN OR ROOTS

During the 1980s protest music emerged known either as Vodun or roots, a mix of Vodun drumming and melody with rock guitar and keyboard. Although this music is based on Vodun musical tradition, it is not necessarily religious music. It is popular music that has attained worldwide recognition and whose lyrics call for social change, and Vodun or roots musicians are committed to upholding Haitian traditions and culture. Boukman Eskperyans is the best known of the bands performing roots. Other notable bands of this genre include Boukan Ginen, Foula, Koudjay, Ram, and Sanba-Yo.

HIP-HOP

Some Haitian-American music, notably hip-hop, has become phenomenally popular among young people in Haiti and the United States. The most famous Haitian hip-hop band to date is the Fugees. Two of the three group members are second-generation Haitian-Americans. The group purposely took its name from a word often used derogatorily to refer to Haitian-Americans—*refugee*—and they wear it proudly. They also refer to their production company and close friends and family as their "refugee camp." At their con-

BOUKMAN ESKPERYANS

Boukman Eskperyans, a music group with wide recognition and acclaim well beyond Haiti's borders, plays a musical genre called Vodun or roots. In it, fast drumming and melody are fused with contemporary rock guitar and keyboard.

A married couple, Mimerose "Manze" and Theodore "Lolo" Beaubrun Jr., founded Boukman Eskperyans in the late 1970s in the small northern town of Ouanaminthe. Today the group boasts seven other members: Maquel Jean-Baptiste, Jean Paul Coffy, Hubert Severe, Henry B. D. Pierre Joseph, Raymond Lexis, Gary Seney, and Hans Dominique.

The name *Boukman* honors Boukman Dutty, the slave and Vodun priest who catalyzed Haiti's slave revolt in 1791. *Eskperyans*, or "experience," refers to the idea that through a religious experience, people can overcome the past and begin anew.

Boukman Eskperyans has used its visibility to promote the legitimacy of Kreyòl as a language and to encourage its use among other Haitian musicians and writers. The lyrics of one of the band's songs cry out, *"Ayisyen-yo, pito pale Franse—Olye yo pale Kreyòl. Se Kreyòl Nou Ye!"* ("Haitians don't speak French, we speak Kreyòl. We are Kreyòl!")

certs, the Fugees perform some raps in Kreyòl to reinforce pride in their Haitian heritage.

That heritage is rich in music and dance. In describing his homeland, the venerable Jean Price-Mars wrote, "I truly believe that one would be justified in defining Haitians as a people who sing and who suffer, who labor and who laugh, who dance and who endure. From cradle to grave, song is associated with one's whole life."[88]

Since the last decades of the twentieth century, Haitians have indeed labored, suffered, and endured. Peasant farmers still put in long hours of arduous work, and many Haitians walk miles daily for water and wood in order to survive in a land upon which Mother Nature no longer smiles. But despite these obstacles, Haiti's artistic and cultural traditions are lively and plentiful. As folklorist Courlander says, "When it is time to dance and sing, nature pours forth spiritual riches from the large end of the horn."[89]

6

FACING THE FUTURE: "BUILDING A NEW NEST"

Petit petit zwaso fe nich.
Little by little a bird builds a nest.
—Edner A. Jeanty and O. Carl Brown,
Parol Granmoun: Haitian Popular Wisdom

Without doubt, Haiti faces immense problems as it steps into the twenty-first century. Poverty, the lack of a stable economy, and the constant drain of its citizens rank among the most pressing concerns. To further complicate these issues, Haiti is divided by its two languages. French is the language of government and commerce, used to communicate with the rest of the world, while Kreyòl is the only language spoken by Haiti's masses, who make up 95 percent of the population. Unfortunately, each problem is linked to other issues. It seems impossible to tackle one problem without first fixing another.

CAN HAITI RECOVER?

Some people even wonder whether recovery is possible at all. One scholar, summarizing a 1995 conference on Haiti, wrote, "How, or whether, it is even possible to create a sustainable, growing economy in a country as ecologically and infrastructurally devastated as Haiti is one of the most challenging and debated issues among scholars and practitioners."[90]

The crux of the problem is trying to stimulate economic growth while coping with the needs of an impoverished population. The Haitian government and people must find a way to balance building roads and communication systems, schools and clinics with the daunting needs of hungry people just trying to make it through the day.

One promising factor is that Haitians are not a people to sit still. Since slave days, they have been feisty and creative and will remain the major shapers of their future. Indeed, they have already begun to do so; activity to remold the future abounds. And in some of these initiatives they are joined by people of goodwill around the globe.

EMBRACING KREYÒL

One of the things Haitians are doing to solve their social and economic problems is embracing their native language and using it as a tool to bring the population closer together.

One step in solving Haiti's social problems is ensuring that everyone can read and write in Kreyòl.

Haitian scholar Jean Price-Mars may have been prophetic when he proclaimed in 1928 that "it is through [Kreyòl] that we can hope to someday close the chasm that makes of us two peoples apparently distinct and often antagonistic."[91]

The first task has been to develop a common written language. Three different spelling systems have been introduced since the 1940s. The latest was developed in 1975 by a Haitian agency, the Institut Pédagogique National (National Pedagogic Institute), following a government mandate to introduce Kreyòl into the nation's schools. (The mandate was later revoked, although many church-run schools do at least some teaching with the instructors speaking Kreyòl.) In 1979 the Haitian government formally recognized this spelling, and today nearly all written Kreyòl uses this system.

Although very few books in Kreyòl exist, the move to teach Haitian children in their own language is a huge step forward in their education. Although schools have tremendous funding and other problems, the use of Kreyòl enables students to understand their teachers and should help decrease the high drop-out rate. Of one hundred rural students who begin school, only three complete the primary grades.

ENHANCING KREYÒL'S STATUS

In an attempt to upgrade the language's status in the eyes of the elite, a few contemporary creative writers are producing their works in Kreyòl. In 1975, for example, Franck Etienne wrote what is considered the first Kreyòl novel, the well-received and respected *Desafi*. He followed this with a drama, *Pèlin Tèt*, which played to about fifty packed audiences in Port-au-Prince in 1978 and 1979 before Jean-Claude "Baby Doc" Duvalier's government shut it down.

The use of Kreyòl also allows impoverished Haitians to participate in the political arena. A radio station operated by the progressive Catholic Church, for instance, broadcast in Kreyòl during the mid-1980s. These broadcasts became vital sources of information for the mostly illiterate masses in the movement to remove Baby Doc from power.

THE CYCLE OF POVERTY

Despite these efforts, though, Kreyòl still has secondary status in Haiti. Until that changes, mastery of French and success in a primarily French-taught school system are still requirements for self-advancement. Although Haitian parents seem willing to make huge sacrifices to send their children to school—paying school fees of up to $25 per month on average annual incomes of $250—the truth is that few young people will make it through school and reach the educational levels needed to break out of poverty.

That cycle of poverty is the largest problem modern Haiti faces today. Three-quarters of the population lives in absolute poverty, and half lacks access to health services. Sixty percent of Haitians live without safe drinking water, and 75 percent lack sanitation facilities. To make matters worse, Haiti's lack of natural resources makes it difficult for the mostly rural population to support itself or get ahead. Furthermore, very few

Some of Haiti's largest problems are the lack of adequate sanitation facilities and little access to safe drinking water.

jobs exist in the cities, and nationwide unemployment has been estimated at anywhere from 50 to 85 percent.

Of the few jobs available, many are assembly-plant jobs in which young women sew clothing from precut pieces. The finished articles are exported to wealthy countries, mainly the United States, rather than sold in Haiti. In 1999 some fifty assembly plants operated in Port-au-Prince, providing jobs to an estimated twenty-five thousand Haitians. However, the wages these workers earn does little to pull them or their families out of poverty.

POOR WORKING CONDITIONS CONTRIBUTE TO THE PROBLEM

These factories are also notorious for their poor working conditions. In 1996 a small group operating out of a tiny office in New York City and calling itself the National Labor Committee, a non-profit educational and advocacy group, investigated conditions in assembly plants in Port-au-Prince. The committee found that the plants were hot, dusty, and poorly lit, with filthy toilets and rats everywhere. The workers said supervisors yelled and cursed at them to make them work faster in an attempt to meet impossibly high production quotas (one worker told of having to attach two hundred collars on T-shirts in an hour). The employees also said sexual harassment was common. Additionally, complaining about pay or conditions, or even taking sick days, could and often did result in losing one's job.

In an attempt to enact change, the National Labor Committee joined forces with a Haitian labor rights group called Batay Ouvriye, which means "Worker's Struggle." Together, these groups launched a campaign to educate worldwide consumers of the conditions under which the Haitian workers labored to produce goods and clothing. The two organizations also sought to expose the corporations responsible for the factories. Although very few changes have actually been made, the coordinators do think their campaign produced some positive results. One activist at Batay Ouvriye spoke of the outcome following their crusade against one prominent American company, Disney:

> "We believe that there are certain things that have been accomplished in spite of [Disney's first negative response]. Many workers now know about [our organization] and

NO FANTASY LAND FOR HAITI'S GARMENT WORKERS

The National Labor Committee (NLC), a small New York-based group that fights for workers' rights in U.S.-owned assembly plants worldwide, investigated conditions in Haitian factories where Walt Disney clothing was produced. In his 1996 "Appeal to Walt Disney Company," committee director Charles Kernaghan described the situation of a Haitian woman working at an assembly plant sewing Disney clothing in Port-au-Prince, whom he had met that year. Kernaghan's report is excerpted from the website of the NLC.

She was a single mother with four young children. They lived in a one room windowless shack, 8 by 11 feet wide, lit by one bare light bulb and with a tin roof that leaked. The room contained: one table, three straight-backed chairs and two small beds. . . . I counted four drinking glasses and three plastic plates. There was no fan, no TV, no radio, no toys, no refrigerator, no stove, no running water. She had to buy water by the bucket and carry it home. The toilet was a hole in the ground, shared with ten other families.

National Labor Committee director Charles Kernaghan speaks out against sweatshops in Haiti.

The children [ages three, eight, eleven, and fourteen] were very small for their age. The mother told us that when she had left for work that morning, she was only able to leave them six gourdes (30 cents). The four children had to feed themselves for the day *on 30 cents—7½ cents per child*. The children had been sent home from school two and a half weeks before because she had been unable to pay their tuition. Tuition for the three older children totaled $2.63 a week, but this was more than the mother earned in a full day sewing Disney shirts. . . .

The mother had years of experience as a sewer. . . . On her assembly line, working furiously under constant pressure, she handled 375 *Pocohantas* shirts an hour—shirts which sell at Wal-Mart for $10.97 each. Yet her average weekly wage was only $10.77!

Workers producing Disney garments in Haiti are thin and tired looking. . . . No one in this [woman's] home had ever seen a Disney movie.

that we support their struggle. When they have problems now, they get in touch with us. The campaign also made us known internationally, so many organizations in other countries contact us, and we keep in touch with them in order to build a stronger solidarity movement.

Even Disney contacted us. They said that they were compiling a report about the problems we raised so they could make changes. They did not make those changes, but there were certain things that indicated that they were sensitive to the points we made in the international campaign.[92]

SPEAKING OUT

Organizing and speaking out are integral to enacting change in any country. In Haiti, another group—the rural peasantry—has begun to do just that. Peasants, still 60 to 70 percent of all Haitians, are organizing into farm co-ops and rural workers unions. Among the largest are the Peasant Movement of Papay and Tèt Kole Ti Peyuizan Ayisyen, which means "Small Haitian Peasants Put Their Heads Together." Within these groups, the peasants identify their common problems and work together to try to solve them. According to researcher and writer Anthony V. Catanese, "Haiti's rural population will no longer quietly and conveniently allow the urban elite to ignore its needs and calls for justice. Rural peasant groups, the primary targets of the more recent and unprecedented political cleansing by the ousted military regime, not only survived their ordeal but gained political strength through steadfastness."[93]

That steadfastness has served them well, and the peasant groups have succeeded in making some minor but important changes. Catanese goes on to say, "The rural majority is now better organized than at any other time in the past and is committed to fighting politically for its rights. In fact, for the first time in Haiti's history, rural Haitians have been freely elected to the national assembly, represent the rural perspective, and reside permanently in rural Haiti."[94]

A CONTINUING EXODUS

Despite these efforts, both rural and urban Haitians continue to face desperate poverty and depleted resources. This situation, as well as Haiti's years of political persecution, have caused many Haitians to seek better lives elsewhere. Although exact figures are difficult to obtain, researchers estimate that as many as 2 million Haitians now live outside of Haiti. Most are in the United States, Canada, and the Dominican Republic, with fewer numbers in the Caribbean, France, and Africa.

This group of Haitians is known either as the diaspora, a term referring to the scattering of a people, or "the tenth department," a term coined in 1990 by then-president Jean-Bertrand Aristide. The tenth department has produced mixed results for Haiti. Because Haiti is among the world's most densely populated nations, emigration helps ease Haiti's population pressure. However, it also causes a "brain drain," depleting the country of its better-educated, more ambitious and resourceful citizens. These people, the ones who opt to leave, are precisely the individuals whom Haiti needs to build its own economy. The exodus represents a vicious circle: Poverty causes enterprising Haitians to leave, making it less likely that Haiti will pull out of poverty and more likely that additional numbers of Haiti's best and brightest will also move to other countries.

Another problem created by the Haitian exodus is that men, especially young men, more often leave than do women or children. Thus, while there may be fewer people in Haiti, those remaining are disproportionately women, children, and the elderly—for the most part, people in greater need of social services such as schools and health care. The absence of men creates an additional burden on women, who already do most of the work in Haiti.

A U.S. Coast Guard patrol stops a boat of Haitian refugees. In an attempt to better their lives, many people leave Haiti by whatever means available.

THE WOMEN'S MOVEMENT

Despite this burden, women in Haiti are remarkably industrious. They are merchants, domestics, factory workers, anything in order to help feed their families. Yet their roles as the primary breadwinners, and as major supporters of the economy, has long been undervalued and even denigrated in Haitian society. Noted Haitian-American novelist Edwidge Dandicat says, "It is estimated that women do two-thirds of the world's work. If this is true, then in Haiti poor women do something like 90 percent of the work, but are the least likely to benefit from the rewards."[95]

The heroic efforts of women who strive to better their families' lives usually go unappreciated by Haitian society.

As a result, a women's rights movement emerged after Baby Doc Duvalier was ousted in 1986. One of its goals was to educate women about their importance to society.

One way to accomplish this, the women soon realized, was to organize into groups determined to improve their situation. The first such group began in the 1980s within the Peasant Movement of Papay (MPP). One woman describes how and why this came to be:

> Women have always been part of MPP, but traditionally we were kept in supportive roles, cooking and cleaning for the men and so on. . . . Now we are able to sit and participate with them in the reflection sessions. We give our opinions, and we make decisions as well. We still have to push this, but we've come a long way, because at first when a woman raised her voice at a meeting, she had to face the possibility that her husband would beat her when she went home. . . .

> For the movement to begin to take hold, women had to decide that we were going to be assertive and start taking part in the decision-making process. We had to do a lot of motivation in both men's and women's groups in order to make that transformation. We worked with men, because men were the greatest obstacle to women's participation, and we had to work with women because many were very shy about assuming new roles since they feared for their relationship with the men.[96]

There are now about a thousand women's groups within the MPP with the goal of helping Haitian women succeed in society. The MPP supports these groups and their social and economic programs, including one that provides credit so that women can borrow money at reasonable interest rates. With the borrowed money, the women undertake projects to generate income or help alleviate their workload. Many recipients raise goats, build corn and grain mills, and establish tree nurseries. The female leaders of the MPP also work to educate women and teach them to read and write, an effort they hope will go a long way toward improving Haiti's situation. One leader points out, though, that "in Haiti where at least three-quarters of the country is illiterate, there is a lot of experience built up over a woman's lifetime, and experience is also a form of education."[97]

"GOD, DO NOT LET ME DIE AS A COWARD"

Tatàn, the founder of a Haitian women's group, describes the police brutality she experienced following the 1991 coup that ousted President Aristide. The 1994 interview is excerpted from *Like the Dew That Waters the Grass: Words from Haitian Women* by Marie M. B. Racine and Kathy Ogle. (In this excerpt, *police* actually refers to government thugs.)

I was arrested on June 10, 1994, while going to obtain a cassette from a radio program series. [I played the cassettes] to tell the women what was going on [with the coup] and to raise their spirits when there was no news on the radio.

Two policemen took me and beat me. I had one big fear. I said to myself, "The cassettes are in this bag I'm carrying! If these guys take it, I'm finished." So the whole time they were hitting me, I held the bag firm in my hand.

When we arrived near the [police headquarters], one of them said, "What are you carrying there?" I had one policeman on each side of me. They were both dressed in black and wore dark glasses. I was praying my heart out. I knew they were going to shoot me anyway, because [their headquarters] already had reports saying I was distributing flyers and putting up posters.

They asked again, "What do you have there?" I said, "I have bought some notebooks for the children I'm teaching." One of them said, "To teach a lesson, eh? I'm going to teach *you* a lesson." He hit me sharply in the back with his knee and I fell forward. I thought both my knees had been broken, but I kept going with my head held high. I kept thinking, "God, do not let me die as a coward."

As we went through the gates of [their headquarters], for some reason one of the guys said, "Let's let this woman go." Then another one pushed me out violently and shouted, "Go on!" As I left, I saw them enter the building.

THE DIASPORA'S ECONOMIC CLOUT

Although women must shoulder heavier workloads when men emigrate, there is a financial benefit to having relatives in other countries. The tenth department sends considerable amounts of money home to relatives. In the 1990s Haitians abroad were sending more than $250 million yearly to family members in Haiti. It is a figure that varies widely: Some estimates put the figure as low as $100 million and others as high as $600 million. Regardless, it amounts to a considerable chunk of Haiti's national budget.

In a country as impoverished as Haiti, this money is essential to many people's survival. Furthermore, one authority believes the funds sent home help individuals "reposition themselves in the hierarchical structure of Haiti,"[98] meaning it helps create greater social mobility and undermines Haiti's rigid class system.

The money also helps effect political change. Since the 1990s, Haitians abroad, for example, have been financially supporting certain candidates for election. Before, Haiti's elite class held a monopoly in influencing political appointments and the very structure of government. The diaspora, though, most of whom live in democratic societies, helps counterbalance the influence of the elites.

According to scholar Michel S. Laguerre,

> The diaspora . . . lends its technical skills to political candidates. . . . In past presidential campaigns, members of the diaspora prepared radio and television advertisements for their preferred candidates. Some members of the diaspora even took leaves of absence from their jobs so that they could return to Haiti and help run the presidential campaigns of their candidates during both the 1990 and 1995 campaigns. They brought with them their technical and organizational skills, their money, and their time.[99]

So, although the diaspora has contributed to a brain drain, the nature of the ongoing relationships Haitians abroad have maintained with their compatriots still on the island has lessened the effects of this loss of human talent. As one scholar says about Haitians and the tenth department, "Together they are writing new chapters in the annals of our [Haitians'] history, and opening new frontiers for our future."[100]

Despite the hardships they face, Haitians look to the future with hope and optimism.

On the surface, Haiti today may appear hopeless, and many people wonder what possible future 7 million impoverished people can have on a barren land. Yet Haitians have a long history of overcoming impossibilities, precisely because of their tenacity and courage. Events of the recent past, since the end of the Duvalier regime in 1986, have forced Haitians to organize and try to seize the reins of their own destinies. No one can guess at Haiti's future, but if it is bright, most people are certain it will be because of the nation's greatest asset: a vibrant and creative people with an unbeatable track record in endurance.

FACTS ABOUT HAITI

GOVERNMENT

Official name: Republic of Haiti (République d'Haiti)

Capital: Port-au-Prince

Political subdivisions: Nine departments

Type of government: Republic

Independence date: January 1, 1804

Legislature: Two-part National Assembly comprising the Senate (twenty-seven seats) and Chamber of Deputies (eighty-three seats)

National flag: Two equal horizontal bands of blue and red with a centered white rectangle bearing the coat of arms, which contains a palm tree flanked by flags and two cannon above a scroll bearing the motto *L'union fait la force* (Union makes strength)

PEOPLE

Population: 7.6 million (1998 estimate)

Distribution: 32% urban; 68% rural (1999 estimate)

Population growth rate: 1.53% (1999 estimate)

Population density: 633 persons per square mile

Life expectancy: At birth: 51.6 years

Male: 49.5 years

Female: 53.9 years

Infant mortality: 97.64 deaths per 1,000 live births (1999 estimate)

Ethnicity: black, 95%; mulatto and white, 5%

Official languages: French and Kreyòl

Literacy rate (for Haitians over age 15): Estimates range from 15% to 53% (1990s)

Religion: Roman Catholic, 80%; Protestant, 16%; Vodun, widely practiced

Net migration rate: -3.26 migrants per 1,000 population (1999 estimate); about 50,000 Haitians emigrate yearly

Population in abject poverty: 75% (1998 estimate)

GEOGRAPHY

Area: 10,714 square miles (27,856 square kilometers)

Coastline: 1,098 miles (1,771 kilometers)

Climate: Tropical; semiarid where mountains in east cut off trade winds; lies in hurricane belt; occasional earthquakes; periodic droughts

Land use: Arable land, 20%; permanent crops, 13%; permanent pastures, 18%; forests and woodland, 5%; other, 44%

Terrain: Mostly rough and mountainous

Borders: Dominican Republic

ECONOMY

Monetary unit: Gourde, equal to 100 centimes

Labor force: 3.6 million (1995 estimate); shortage of skilled labor but unskilled labor abundant; agriculture, 66%; services, 25%; industry, 9%

Annual inflation rate (consumer prices): 8% (1998 estimate)

Average annual per capita income: $410 (1998 estimate)

Unemployment rate: 60% (1996 estimate)

Natural resources: None

Exports: $110 million (1997 estimate); light manufactures, 80.5%; coffee, 7.6%; other agriculture, 7.2%

Imports: $486 million (1997 estimate), machines and manufactured goods, 50%; food and beverages, 39%; petroleum products, 2%; chemicals, 5%; fats and oils, 4%

Major trading partners: United States and European Union

Debt owed to other countries and foreign institutions: $1 billion (1997 estimate)

Agricultural products: Coffee, mangoes, sugarcane, rice, corn, sorghum, wood

Industries (based on imported parts): Sugar refining, textiles, flour milling, cement, tourism, light assembly

NOTES

CHAPTER 1: LAND AND PEOPLE

1. Quoted in Robert Debs Heinl Jr. and Nancy Gordon Heinl, *Written in Blood: The Story of the Haitian People, 1492–1971.* Boston: Houghton Mifflin, 1978, p. 3.

2. Wade Davis, *The Serpent and the Rainbow.* New York: Warner Books, 1985, p. 40.

3. James G. Leyburn, *The Haitian People.* 1941. Reprint, Westport, CT: Greenwood, 1980, p. 291.

4. Heinl and Heinl, *Written in Blood*, p. 569.

5. U.S. Central Intelligence Agency, *World Factbook, 1999: Haiti.* www.odci.gov/cia/publications/factbook/ha.html.

6. Herbert Gold, *Best Nightmare on Earth: A Life in Haiti.* New York: Prentice-Hall, 1991, p. 15.

7. Heinl and Heinl, *Written in Blood*, p. 4.

8. Amy Wilentz, *The Rainy Season: Haiti Since Duvalier.* New York: Simon and Schuster, 1989, p. 246.

9. Davis, *The Serpent and the Rainbow*, p. 50.

10. Davis, *The Serpent and the Rainbow*, p. 40.

11. Quoted in Robert I. Rotberg, ed., *Haiti Renewed: Political and Economic Prospects.* Washington, DC: Brookings Institution, 1997, p. 4.

12. Quoted in Rotberg, *Haiti Renewed: Political and Economic Prospects*, p. 4.

CHAPTER 2: FROM SLAVERY TO INDEPENDENT REPUBLIC: THE 1500s TO 1800s

13. Christopher Columbus, *The Log of Christopher Columbus*, trans. Robert H. Fuson. Camden, ME: International Marine, 1987, pp. 136–37.

14. Quoted in Catherine A. Sunshine and Deborah Menkart, eds., *Teaching About Haiti.* Washington, DC: Network of Educators on the Americas, 1993, p. 5.

15. Heinl and Heinl, *Written in Blood*, p. 19.

16. Leyburn, *The Haitian People*, p. 15.

17. Carolyn E. Fick, *The Making of Haiti: The Saint Domingue Revolution from Below*. Knoxville: University of Tennessee Press, 1990, p. 35.

18. Fick, *The Making of Haiti*, p. 34.

19. Quoted in Fick, *The Making of Haiti*, p. 33.

20. Heinl and Heinl, *Written in Blood*, p. 29.

21. Quoted in Heinl and Heinl, *Written in Blood*, p. 37.

22. Davis, *The Serpent and the Rainbow*, p. 245.

23. Davis, *The Serpent and the Rainbow*, p. 246.

24. Heinl and Heinl, *Written in Blood*, p. 60.

25. Leyburn, *The Haitian People*, p. 27.

26. Heinl and Heinl, *Written in Blood*, p. 101.

27. Heinl and Heinl, *Written in Blood*, p. 102.

28. Quoted in Heinl and Heinl, *Written in Blood*, p. 108.

29. Quoted in Heinl and Heinl, *Written in Blood*, pp. 108–109.

30. Fick, *The Making of Haiti*, pp. 215–16.

31. Fick, *The Making of Haiti*, p. 221.

32. Quoted in Heinl and Heinl, *Written in Blood*, p. 299.

CHAPTER 3: MODERN HAITI'S
UNSETTLED POLITICAL ORDER

33. Heinl and Heinl, *Written in Blood*, pp. 352–53.

34. Hans Schmidt, *The United States Occupation of Haiti, 1915–1934*. New Brunswick, NJ: Rutgers University Press, 1971, p. 60.

35. Quoted in Heinl and Heinl, *Written in Blood*, p. 396.

36. Quoted in Schmidt, *The United States Occupation of Haiti, 1915–1934*, p. 84.

37. Schmidt, *The United States Occupation of Haiti, 1915–1934*, p. 101.

38. Quoted in Schmidt, *The United States Occupation of Haiti, 1915–1934*, p. 102.

39. Quoted in Heinl and Heinl, *Written in Blood*, p. 452.

40. Quoted in Schmidt, *The United States Occupation of Haiti, 1915–1934*, p. 105.

41. Wilentz, *The Rainy Season*, p. 41.

42. Schmidt, *The United States Occupation of Haiti, 1915–1934*, p. 230.

43. Quoted in Schmidt, *The United States Occupation of Haiti, 1915–1934*, p. 233.

44. Quoted in Leyburn, *The Haitian People*, p. xiv.

45. Elizabeth Abbott, *Haiti: The Duvaliers and Their Legacy*. New York: Simon and Schuster, 1988, p. 65.

46. Abbott, *Haiti*, p. 78.

47. Quoted in Heinl and Heinl, *Written in Blood*, p. 601.

48. Abbott, *Haiti*, p. 98.

49. Abbott, *Haiti*, p. 110.

50. Quoted in Heinl and Heinl, *Written in Blood*, p. 651.

51. Wilentz, *The Rainy Season*, p. 42.

52. Cindy Poppen and Scott Wright, eds., *Beyond the Mountains, More Mountains: Haiti Faces the Future*. Washington, DC: EPICA and Voices for Haiti, 1994, p. 8.

53. Abbott, *Haiti*, p. 370.

54. Mark Danner, "The Fall of the Prophet," *New York Review*, December 2, 1993, p. 45.

55. Catherine Orenstein, "Haiti Undone," *NACLA Report on the Americas*, November/December 1999, pp. 10–12.

56. David Gonzalez, "Haiti's Long-Delayed Election Is Chaotic but Nonviolent," *New York Times*, May 22, 2000, p. A4.

CHAPTER 4: DAILY LIFE IN HAITI

57. Quoted in Poppen and Wright, *Beyond the Mountains, More Mountains*, p. 23.

58. Leyburn, *The Haitian People*, p. 97.

59. Leyburn, *The Haitian People*, p. 194.

60. Fred J. Hay, introduction to *When Night Falls, Kric? Krac!: Haitian Folktales*, by Liliane Nérette Louis. Englewood, CO: Libraries Unlimited, 1999, p. 23.

61. Quoted in Marie M. B. Racine and Kathy Ogle, *Like the Dew That Waters the Grass: Words from Haitian Women*. Washington, DC: EPICA, 1999, p. 61.

62. Wilentz, *The Rainy Season*, pp. 17–18.

63. Quoted in Racine and Ogle, *Like the Dew That Waters the Grass*, p. 101.

64. Quoted in Linda Goyette, "Haiti's Invisible Servants," *Edmonton (Alberta) Journal*, March 20, 1999, p. F2.

65. Quoted in Linda Goyette, "A Land of Hope and Endurance," *Edmond (Alberta) Journal*, March 21, 1999, p. F5.

66. Quoted in Goyette, "A Land of Hope and Endurance," p. F5.

67. Leyburn, *The Haitian People*, p. 135.

68. Davis, *The Serpent and the Rainbow*, p. 76.

69. Quoted in Sunshine and Menkart, *Teaching About Haiti*, p. 38.

70. Quoted in Racine and Ogle, *Like the Dew That Waters the Grass*, p. 165.

71. Wilentz, *The Rainy Season*, pp. 274–75.

CHAPTER 5: HAITIAN ARTS AND MUSIC

72. Brian Weinstein and Aaron Segal, *Haiti: Political Failures, Cultural Successes*. New York: Praeger, 1984, p. ix.

73. Edner A. Jeanty and O. Carl Brown, *Parol Granmoun: Haitian Popular Wisdom*. Port-au-Prince: Editions Learning Center, 1976, p. x.

74. Jean Price-Mars, *Ainsi Parla L'Oncle . . . Essais D'ethnographie*. Port-au-Prince: Imprimerie de Compiegne, 1928, p. 5.

75. Quoted in Hay, introduction to *When Night Falls, Kric? Krac!*, p. 31.

76. Price-Mars, *Ainsi Parla L'Oncle*, pp. 9–10.

77. Heinl and Heinl, *Written in Blood*, p. 557.

78. Quoted in Ute Stebich, *Haitian Art*. Brooklyn, NY: Brooklyn Museum, 1978, pp. 14–15.

79. Quoted in Stebich, *Haitian Art*, p. 15.

80. Quoted in Stebich, *Haitian Art*, p. 15.

81. Selden Rodman, *Where Art Is Joy—Haitian Art: The First Forty Years*. New York: Ruggles de Latour, 1988, p. 13.

82. Rodman, *Where Art Is Joy*, p. 19.

83. Rodman, *Where Art Is Joy*, p. 221.

84. Quoted in J. P. Slavin, "Enock Placide: Expression over Tradition," *HAITI Insight: A Bulletin on Refugee and Human Rights Affairs*, January/February 1998, pp. 1, 8.

85. Quoted in Nina Jaffe, *A Voice for the People: The Life and Work of Harold Courlander.* New York: Henry Holt, 1997, p. 25.

86. Leyburn, *The Haitian People*, p. 153.

87. Davis, *The Serpent and the Rainbow*, pp. 115–16.

88. Price-Mars, *Ainsi Parla L'Oncle*, pp. 18–19.

89. Quoted in Jaffe, *A Voice for the People*, p. 25.

CHAPTER 6: FACING THE FUTURE: "BUILDING A NEW NEST"

90. Quoted in Rotberg, *Haiti Renewed*, p. 6.

91. Price-Mars, *Ainsi Parla L'Oncle*, p. 17.

92. Quoted in Racine and Ogle, *Like the Dew That Waters the Grass*, p. 109.

93. Quoted in Rotberg, *Haiti Renewed*, pp. 191–92.

94. Quoted in Rotberg, *Haiti Renewed*, p. 192.

95. Quoted in Racine and Ogle, *Like the Dew That Waters the Grass*, p. 3.

96. Quoted in Racine and Ogle, *Like the Dew That Waters the Grass*, p. 71.

97. Quoted in Racine and Ogle, *Like the Dew That Waters the Grass*, p. 62.

98. Quoted in Rotberg, *Haiti Renewed*, p. 177.

99. Quoted in Rotberg, *Haiti Renewed*, p. 172.

100. Gérard Alphonse Férère, "Haiti and Its Diaspora: New Historical, Cultural, and Economic Frontiers," Haiti On Line, August 27, 1999. www.haitionline.com/1999/11021.html# DIASPORA.

GLOSSARY

bambouche: A social dance without religious significance.

bidonville: A slum or shantytown.

buccan: From a Carib term for smoked meat, it became the basis for the name *buccaneers,* referring to French hunters on Tortuga Island and in northwest Hispaniola who learned this technique of preserving meat from surviving Carib peoples.

Boukman Eksperyans: A widely acclaimed Haitian band of Vodun or root music, which upholds Haitian traditions and protests injustices.

bula: The smallest of the three Vodun drums; also known as *kata.*

Cacos: Peasant soldiers, often recruited for a specific cause, who operated in Haiti off and on since 1867 using guerrilla-style tactics and who mounted resistance against the 1915 U.S. occupation under Charlemagne Péralte.

clairin: A cheap rum.

corvée: Forced labor on roads required by law; imposed under U.S. occupation.

diaspora: The approximately 2 million Haitians who live outside of Haiti.

gourde (*goud*): Haiti's monetary currency.

Hispaniola: The Caribbean island shared by Haiti and the Dominican Republic.

hounfor: A Vodun temple; a simple structure with an earthen floor.

houngan: A Vodun priest; from the Fon words *oun,* meaning "spirits," and *gan,* meaning, "chief."

kompa: Popular music that originated in Haiti in the 1950s; similar to merengue but with a slower tempo and simplified melodies.

Kreyòl: The language spoken by Haitians.

krik? krak!: The traditional question and answer used to establish that a storyteller is ready to begin and the audience is ready to listen.

lakou: A horseshoe-shaped compound or courtyard in rural areas in which various households of an extended family live.

lwa: A Vodun deity or spirit.

mambo: A Vodun priestess. In Haiti, *mambos* are powerful individuals, both socially and spiritually.

manman: The largest of the three Vodun drums.

maquila: A factory owned by a foreigner in which assembly of imported parts or pieces takes place.

Maroons: Runaway slaves who formed disciplined communities in Haiti's mountainous regions.

merengue: The national music and dance style of Haiti, similar to that of the Dominican Republic.

morne: A mountain.

mulatto: A person of mixed African and white ancestry.

plasaj: Polygynous unions in which the man's wives do not live together but are "placed" near the man's various fields in the countryside.

polygynous: A term referring to a man with two or more wives.

primitive: One of several names given to the unschooled artists—and their style of painting who emerged with the opening of the Centre d'Art in 1944.

rara: Bands of people in costumes and masks who cavort through the streets during Mardi Gras, or Carnival, performing often lewd dances.

restavecs: Unpaid child domestic laborers sent from impoverished rural homes to work in urban homes in exchange for food and lodging.

Saint Domingue: The French name for the colony that eventually became Haiti.

seconde: The medium-size drum of the three Vodun drums.

Taíno: An indigenous group inhabiting Hispaniola at the time of Christopher Columbus's arrival in the New World.

tap-tap: A colorfully decorated Haitian bus, so named because passengers tap on the side when they want to get off.

tenth department: A name, with political overtones, applied to the estimated 2 million Haitians now living abroad; see also diaspora.

Ti Legliz: Literally "Little Church," the Roman Catholic Church movement in which people gather together to study the Bible and apply it to their own situations.

tonnelle: An outdoor canopy consisting of a roof of boughs and leaves supported by uprights; used for Vodun dances.

Tonton Macoutes: Former president François Duvalier's private militia.

vaccine: Hollowed bamboo used as a musical instrument.

Vodun: The religion of Haiti's majority, in which the believer tries to remain in harmony with the spirits. The spirits, or *lwa*, communicate with humans through a spiritual possession of their minds and bodies.

Vodun or roots music: Haitian protest music that emerged in the 1980s, combining Vodun drumming with rock guitar.

Windward Passage: The channel between Hispaniola and Cuba; a sea route whose location was formerly strategic.

CHRONOLOGY

1492
Christopher Columbus lands on Hispaniola; he encounters native Taíno Arawak people.

1697
Spain cedes the western portion of Hispaniola to France, which calls it Saint Domingue.

1720s
French settlers discover Saint Domingue's rich soil and stake out plantations.

1766–1791
Saint Domingue reigns as the world's wealthiest colony.

1791
Slave revolt commences.

1793
Slave rebellion is successfully concluded; Toussaint-Louverture becomes the first leader of the freed slaves.

1802
The War of Independence begins after Napoléon's sixty-seven-ship armada arrives in Saint Domingue.

1803
Napoléon surrenders to Haiti's former slaves after sixty thousand French soldiers perish.

1804
Dessalines declares Saint Domingue's independence, renaming the nation Haiti.

1807
Haiti is divided; Christophe rules in the north while Pétion rules in the south.

1820
The country reunifies without struggle under President Boyer.

1915
U.S. Marines occupy Haiti.

1919
Marines kill Caco resistance leader Charlemagne Péralte.

1934
U.S. Marines withdraw from Haiti.

1957
François Duvalier is elected president.

1964
Duvalier proclaims himself president for life.

1971
Duvalier names his only son, Jean-Claude, nicknamed Baby Doc, as his successor.

1985
Tens of thousands of Haitians march in protest of the Duvalier regime.

1986
Baby Doc and his family are exiled to Paris; General Henri Namphy is named head of the provisional government.

1988
Macoutes attack and burn Father Jean-Bertrand Aristide's church; soldiers oust Namphy; General Prosper Avril assumes leadership.

1990
Aristide enters the presidential race; wins by landslide in Haiti's first free and fair election.

1991
An army coup overthrows Aristide, installs General Raoul Cédras, and unleashes reign of terror against democratic movement; refugees pour out of Haiti.

1994
UN Security Council authorizes the United States to restore Aristide to power.

1996
René Préval becomes president in an election in which only 15 percent of the electorate votes.

2000
Haitians reaffirm commitment to democratic process in May, with more than 45 percent of the electorate voting in nonviolent elections for thousands of legislators and local officials; presidential elections are scheduled for November.

SUGGESTIONS FOR FURTHER READING

BOOKS

Jean-Bertrand Aristide, *In the Parish of the Poor: Writings from Haiti.* Trans. and ed. Amy Wilentz. Maryknoll, NY: Orbis Books, 1990. In an open letter to Christians in Latin America who have struggled alongside the poor, Aristide recounts his own experiences—including various attempts on his life—as a priest in a seething Port-au-Prince shantytown.

Jean-Robert Cadet, *Restavec: From Haitian Slave Child to Middle-Class American.* Austin: University of Texas Press, 1998. The heart-rending autobiography of a former *restavec.*

Francine Jacobs, *The Tainos: The People Who Welcomed Columbus.* New York: G. P. Putnam's Sons, 1992. A fascinating account of these forgotten people and the tragedy that befell them.

Nina Jaffe, *A Voice for the People: The Life and Work of Harold Courlander.* New York: Henry Holt, 1997. An informative biography of a folklorist who collected music and dance from many cultures, including Haiti.

Liliane Nérette Louis, *When Night Falls, Kric? Krac!: Haitian Folktales.* Ed. Fred J. Hay. Englewood, CO: Libraries Unlimited, 1999. A collection of twenty-nine tales, with a general introduction to Haiti by the editor that helps set the stories in their context.

Cindy Poppen and Scott Wright, eds., *Beyond the Mountains, More Mountains: Haiti Faces the Future.* Washington, DC: EPICA and Voices for Haiti, 1994. A report on post-Duvalier Haiti emphasizing the popular movement for change and the forces seeking to silence it.

Marie M. B. Racine and Kathy Ogle, *Like the Dew That Waters the Grass: Words from Haitian Women.* Washington, DC: EPICA, 1999. Haitian women from all walks of life share their stories and struggles.

Selden Rodman, *Where Art Is Joy. Haitian Art: The First Forty Years.* New York: Ruggles de Latour, 1988. A comprehensive overview of Haitian art, from the 1944 opening of the Centre d'Art through the 1980s, by an individual instrumental in promoting Haitian art and artists during this period. Contains striking color plates and black-and-white illustrations. It places more emphasis on the artists' personalities and historical circumstances than Ute Stebich's *Haitian Art*, which focuses more on analyzing the content and composition of the artists' work.

Ute Stebich, *Haitian Art.* Brooklyn, NY: Brooklyn Museum, 1978. A beautiful volume of Haitian art, with an emphasis on the paintings created after the 1944 founding of the Centre d'Art. The author explains the art pieces and their creators, with their roots both in Haiti's isolation and the Vodun religion.

Frances Temple, *Taste of Salt: A Story of Modern Haiti.* New York: HarperCollins, 1992. In this fictional account, two teens active in Aristide's movement for social change get to know one another as they recount their experiences and the persecution they endured following the coup d'etat.

Albert Valdman, *Ann Pale Kreyòl: An Introductory Course in Haitian Creole.* Bloomington: Indiana University Press, 1988. This course contains written and recorded materials to give the beginner basic tools for understanding and speaking Kreyòl.

Amy Wilentz, *The Rainy Season: Haiti Since Duvalier.* New York: Simon and Schuster, 1989. An engaging personal account of the turbulent post-Duvalier years by a journalist who introduces and follows a memorable cast of characters.

PERIODICALS

Faces: The Magazine About People, February 1992. (The entire issue is dedicated to Haiti.)

Websites

Association for Haitian American Development, (www.aha-kreyol.org). This is the website of an Atlanta-based organization that seeks to present a Haitian viewpoint about Haiti in contrast to the many negative images portrayed in the mass media. It provides links to more than eighty-five sites (universities, organizations, media, travel, art and literature, and more) on Haiti.

Boukman Eksperyans (www.boukman.com/>). This musical group advocates social change while promoting pride in traditional Haitian culture and language. The website contains photos, an upcoming tour schedule, and an introduction to the group and its philosophy.

Haitian News & Links (www.greatbasin.net/~networth/haiti/news.htm). Contains dozens of links to Haiti-related sites.

Haiti Forum (www.haitiforum.com/). This beautiful animated site, which promotes Haiti and Haitian culture and is sponsored by the California Service and Information Network, has won many awards. It includes a basic illustrated history of Haiti, recipes, poetry, and a glossary of Haitian mythological (Vodun) terms.

Kreyòl (www.kreyol.com/). A substantial dictionary of English-to-Kreyòl and Kreyòl-to-English words and terms, edited by Hertz Nazaire.

National Labor Committee (www.nlcnet.org). Contains detailed reports on this organization's investigations into assembly-plant factory conditions in Haiti.

Planet Haiti (www.geocities.com/Heartland/Ranch/9178/). Colorful "tourist" photos take visitors on a tour of four Haitian cities. It also provides information on Haitian history, statistics, and links.

WORKS CONSULTED

BOOKS

Elizabeth Abbott, *HAITI: The Duvaliers and Their Legacy*. New York: Simon and Schuster, 1988. A thorough, highly readable account of the devastating Duvalier regimes, based on abundant interviews with survivors.

Jean-Bertrand Aristide with Christophe Wargny, *Jean-Bertrand Aristide: An Autobiography*. Trans. Linda M. Maloney. Maryknoll, NY: Orbis Books, 1993. The popular Haitian leader's own story, with his unique perspective on Haiti's current situation.

Christopher Columbus, *The Log of Christopher Columbus*. Trans. Robert H. Fuson. Camden, ME: International Marine, 1987. Columbus's own record and observations on his first voyages to the New World, written for the Spanish monarchs.

Harold Courlander, *The Drum and the Hoe: Life and Lore of the Haitian People*. Berkeley and Los Angeles: University of California Press, 1960. A collection of Haitian lore, including dance, folktales, and children's games, with a special emphasis on musical instruments and songs.

Wade Davis, *Passage of Darkness: The Ethnobiology of the Haitian Zombie*. Chapel Hill: University of North Carolina Press, 1988. An extended, more scholarly version of *The Serpent and the Rainbow*.

——, *The Serpent and the Rainbow*. New York: Warner Books, 1985. An entertaining best-seller written for the general public on this ethnobotanist's investigation into the phenomenon of zombies.

Carolyn E. Fick, *The Making of Haiti: The Saint Domingue Revolution from Below*. Knoxville: University of Tennessee Press, 1990. This scholarly text presents Haiti's revolution from the slaves' vantage point, by using many original sources.

Herbert Gold, *Best Nightmare on Earth: A Life in Haiti.* New York: Prentice-Hall, 1991. Personal anecdotes about Gold's time in Haiti—mixed with history, politics, and musings about Haitian culture—create an insightful account.

Robert Debs Heinl Jr. and Nancy Gordon Heinl, *Written in Blood: The Story of the Haitian People, 1492–1971.* Boston: Houghton Mifflin, 1978. A highly detailed, well-documented, comprehensive history covering the period indicated.

Edner A. Jeanty and O. Carl Brown, *Parol Granmoun: Haitian Popular Wisdom.* Port-au-Prince: Editions Learning Center, 1976. A collection of 999 Haitian proverbs, with short introductory essays by the compilers.

Marion F. Lansing, *Liberators and Heroes of the West Indian Islands.* Boston: L. C. Page, 1953. One chapter is devoted to a biography of Toussaint-Louverture and another to "Founders of Haiti," including Dessalines, Christophe, and Pétion.

James G. Leyburn, *The Haitian People.* 1941. Reprint, Westport, CT: Greenwood, 1980. A highly regarded, authoritative "primer" on Haitian culture and history, with an emphasis on the role of class.

David Nicholls, *Haiti in Caribbean Context: Ethnicity, Economy, and Revolt.* Houndmills, England: Macmillan, 1985. An academic investigation into the relationship between race and economics in Haiti and neighboring islands.

Jean Price-Mars, *Ainsi Parla L'Oncle . . . Essais D'ethnographic.* Port-au-Prince. Imprimerie de Compiegne, 1928. A groundbreaking, much-quoted work exploring and lauding Haiti's African roots, written by a Haitian scholar.

Robert I. Rotberg, ed., *Haiti Renewed: Political and Economic Prospects.* Washington, DC: Brookings Institution, 1997. A collection of thirteen essays analyzing Haiti's contemporary problems and proposing policies or approaches that might help solve them.

Hans Schmidt, *The United States Occupation of Haiti, 1915–1934.* New Brunswick, NJ: Rutgers University Press, 1971. Extensive use of primary sources and colorful quotes draws the reader into this traumatic chapter of Haitian history.

Catherine A. Sunshine and Deborah Menkart, eds., *Teaching About Haiti*. Washington, DC: Network of Educators on the Americas, 1993. Geared to secondary-school teachers, this guide to contemporary Haiti is a rich potpourri of analytical and background articles, folktales, proverbs, and resources for action and information.

Brian Weinstein and Aaron Segal, *Haiti: Political Failures, Cultural Successes*. New York: Praeger, 1984. A scholarly treatment of the economic, ecological, and political challenges facing Haiti and a tribute to the country's enduring culture.

Emily Will, ed., with contributers Sharon Wyse Miller and Rhonda Miller, *Haiti: Teacher's Guide*. Akron, PA: Mennonite Central Committee, 1996. A compilation of teaching activities, including stories, cooking activities, and Haitian games for teachers working with grades one through eight. Part of a larger Latin American/Caribbean learning and activity box.

Michelle Wucker, *Why the Cocks Fight: Dominicans, Haitians, and the Struggle for Hispaniola*. New York: Hill & Wang, 1999. A thorough investigation into and analysis of the mostly rocky history of Dominican and Haitian relationships.

PERIODICALS

Mark Danner, "The Fall of the Prophet," *New York Review*, December 2, 1993.

David Gonzalez, "Haiti's Long-Delayed Election Is Chaotic but Nonviolent," *New York Times*, May 22, 2000.

Linda Goyette, "Haiti's Invisible Servants," *Edmonton (Alberta) Journal*, March 20, 1999.

———, "A Land of Hope and Endurance," *Edmonton (Alberta) Journal*, March 21, 1999.

Jean Jean-Pierre, "The Tenth Department," *NACLA Report on the Americas*, January/February 1994.

Anthony Ng, "The Fugees: Hip-Hop's Haitian-American Pioneers," *HAITI Insight: A Bulletin on Refugee and Human Rights Affairs*, June/July 1996.

Catherine Orenstein, "Haiti Undone," *NACLA Report on the Americas*, November/December 1999.

J. P. Slavin, "Enock Placide: Expression over Tradition," *HAITI Insight: A Bulletin on Refugee and Human Rights Affairs*, January/February 1998.

Internet Sources

Alix Cantave, "Political and Economic Reconstruction of Haiti." June 1996. www.haitionline.com/1999/11021.htm #DIASPORA.

Jace Clayton, "Compas," 1999. www.africana.com/tt_030.htm.

Gérard Alphonse Férère, "Haiti and Its Diaspora: New Historical, Cultural, and Economic Frontiers," Haiti On Line, August 27, 1999. www.haitionline.com/1999/11021.htm #DIASPORA.

Charles Kernaghan, "An Appeal to Walt Disney Company," May 29, 1996. www.nlcnet.org/Disney/Disapp.htm.

U.S. Central Intelligence Agency, *World Factbook, 1999: Haiti.* www.odci.gov/cia/publications/factbook/ha.html.

Eric Verhoogen, "The U.S. in Haiti: How to Get Rich on Eleven Cents an Hour," January 1996. www.nlcnet.org/Haiti11.htm.

INDEX

PICTURE CREDITS

ABOUT THE AUTHOR

Emily Wade Will, currently a freelance writer, resides in Lancaster County, Pennsylvania. She has lived in Jamaica and Mexico and has traveled widely in Latin America. She holds a master's degree in agricultural journalism from the University of Wisconsin at Madison and has worked as a journalist.